THE RISE OF MIDDLE CLASSES IN MANIPUR

The Rise of Middle Classes in Manipur

Edited by

Professor Gangmumei Kamei

AKANSHA PUBLISHING HOUSE
NEW DELHI • GUWAHATI • VISAKHAPATNAM

AKANSHA PUBLISHING HOUSE
4649-B/21, Ansari Road
Daryaganj, New Delhi-110002
Phones: 23268193, 09435116718
Email: ektabooks@yahoo.com
visit us: www.akanshapublishinghouse.com

The Rise of Middle Classes in Manipur

First Published 2012

ISBN 978-81-8370-323-9

PRINTED IN INDIA

Published by Akansha Publishing House, New Delhi-110002 and printed at Harmain Offset Printers, Delhi.

CONTENTS

FOREWORD

Mainland India, to use a construct that signifies both a geography and a politics and has a widespread usage in India's North East, has to, and does, try and understand the sense of grievance and discontent that is present in the region. To do so it has had to delve into the history and culture of the area, investigate the energies of its economy, map the working of law and the legal system, and study the dynamics of interest and power that drive its politics. It has to do so while developing an interdisciplinary sensibility. It needs scholarly help.

The edited collection by Professor Gangmumei Kamei on the *Rise of Middle Classes in Manipur* is an extremely valuable input into this understanding of a complex region. By looking at an understudied area it adds a great deal to our knowledge of a troubled and strategic border state that has been the site of considerable social and political conflict. The book's value also lies in the contribution it makes to the comparative literature on the middle class, a segment of society that has been neglected by the social sciences community in India. It is one that contains within itself many clues on the future trajectory of the country, since the middle class is both an identifiable social segment and a social aspiration. This needs to be recognized. We therefore need to study the middle class from several directions by using different analytical tools, and in response to innovative questions especially concerning modernity, if we are to seriously understand the processes of change, especially under globalization, that are transforming all societies in the world today. The internal composition of this class and its external location and bearing, with respect to other classes, needs to be mapped. The book should thus be regarded as the first attempt in this exercise of mapping, an aid that helps us unpack the role of the middle class in making the future of India's North East. In many scholarly circles the middle class of the region is regarded as a conundrum.

In this brief foreword let me set out what I see as some of the features of the middle class that need to be empirically examined and theoretically debated. The initial question of such an exercise is the conceptual relationship between the concepts of 'petty bourgeoisie' and the 'middle class'. Although each concept is located within a different analytical framework we need to examine their similarities and dissimilarities, in terms of what work they do in the conceptual schema, since both are regarded as playing a particular role as historical agents of change. It is this role that helps us understand statements such as 'the petty bourgeoisie was not strong enough to prevent the continued rule of the Junkers in the last decades of the 19th Century in Germany and hence the power of the state remained with a class that was out of step with the processes of history' or 'a new petty bourgeoisie is appearing among the Dalit community thereby producing a new politics of presence in the public domain'. The big question for the North East is to understand the processes that produce the petty bourgeoisie and to see what role this new social group has played in the shaping of the contemporary in the last six decades. Differentiating between the petty bourgeoisie and the middle class is hence of importance for a historical sociology.

Since the production and reproduction of the middle class has been going on for many decades now knowing more about its internal dynamics and its external constraints would be of help if we are to address the question: In what way is it a historical agent of change in the North East? There are several aspects that can be probed in pursuit of this question such as the extent of its educational attainment, the nature and capabilities for social leadership that it displays, the quality and direction of its political practice towards its own society and also towards the larger region and the mainland, the attitude that its members adopt towards modernity, and, in this period of globalization, its location at all levels of the economy whether these be local, regional, and national. As a historical agent we need to know how the middle class in the North East region navigates its agency between the two banks that determine its choices of culture and economy.

To investigate this role of the middle class I want, somewhat ambitiously, to offer three propositions that are worth investigating. The first concerns its experiential location. Because of this particular social location, which is marked by experiences of a distinct kind, the middle class is progressive in its attitude towards matters of culture. It therefore leads the interaction between the old cultural order and the new and serves as the harbinger of modernity in society. It sees such modernity as an opportunity for self-advancement, as a chance to enter the future and overcome some of the constraints that it faces in the present. It therefore develops a capability to be hybrid and ambidextrous. This leads to the second proposition that the middle class, because it is receptive to ideas, is innovative in its disposition. This innovativeness translates into an important driver of social change. Mapping the role of the middle class would require mapping this innovative disposition. The third is that the middle class is mostly conservative in politics since it, having arrived, does not want to change the existing order. It willingly gets co-opted by the structures of power and then becomes an effective spokesperson for this old order. Incremental change is preferred to radical change.

Framing propositions at this level invites us to engage with the difficult question of what is the structural location of this class in a society. Does it have common features, across societies, or is it a 'cluster idea' that allows for both individual agency and collective action, the latter being more discernible as compared to the former in terms of its social signature? Elaborating on the concept of the middle class as a cluster idea has promised because we need to understand the internal relation between the individual and the collective, and the significance of this relation for historical agency, for positioning itself as a 'class' that acts to promote certain outcomes within the system of power in society. These are questions at some remove from the empirical study but they need to be considered if we are to examine the role of the middle class as a historical agent. The North East of India requires such consideration. As does the mainland. This book on the middle class in Manipur is a small beginning and will, I hope, inspire more such studies of the region.

Peter Ronald deSouza
Director
Indian Institute of Advanced Study,
Shimla.

PREFACE

It is considered that there is a gap in the understanding of the role of Middle Classes in Manipur. In the month of September, 2011 a one day symposium was organized under the aegis of Centre for Social Studies (proposed) at Imphal on the subject. We invited some scholars of Social Sciences to present their papers on the subject. We also requested Professor Ghanshyam Shah, National Fellow in the Indian Institute of Advanced Study at Shimla. He was kind enough to send a brief note which was the talking point of the symposium. The participants of the symposium are named among the contributors to whom I am extremely grateful. The eight papers published in the small book have done justice to the subject. Professor Kshetri Bimola presided over the symposium and contributed a paper.

I am grateful to Professor Peter deSouza Director of the Indian Institute of Advanced Study, Shimla who on my request wrote a worthy Foreword to this work. I am happy that Mr. M.P. Misra, the CMD of the Akansha Publishing House, New Delhi published the book. I am also grateful to the contributors for offering me the editorship of this publication.

Gangmumei Kamei

1

MIDDLE CLASS

Ghanshyam Shah

All concepts are constructed and deconstructed by scholars and activists in different context, time and their perspective as well as purpose. The concept may change from time to time with the purpose of analysis: What one wants to answer/inquire. This is also true for the concept 'middle class'. Hence there is and cannot be one the meaning.

Generally in the Marxist framework the class analysis is in the context of mode of production. Position of each group of people is related to one's position in mode of production, relationship of production. Those who own means of production which employ others as workers for production and the owners take away surplus are capitalist. And the workers who sell labour, add value to the commodity but do not get benefit of the surplus that they generate are proletariats or workers. The rest between these two classes who do not physically labour and involve directly in material production who are involved in managing and exchanging the product in the market, who work as intellectuals are petty-bourgeois or middle class.

However in Weberian's sense Class is related to social stratification. For him social class and status or honour are basis of social stratification indicating social differences. In this power and domination are important components to identify differences. So for Marx class is primarily economic category around conflict of interests, for Weber it is around social status and power.

Marxist classifies objective situation of class in term of position in production relationship and subjective nature of class–consciousness. A labourer is objectively labour but he may not be conscious of his position as labourer and his exploitation. The former is class in itself and later is class for itself. In our situation more often than not a person from upper Caste working in factory as worker would like to identify as middle class person than working class. Here cultural factor play important role in determining class consciousness.

Objectively for descriptive purpose middle class may be identified on the basis of occupation. Generally they are professionals and white collar employees. They are engaged in non-manual work. Another way of defining middle class in terms of income. The criteria of income vary from time to time and context to context. Some scholars combine occupation and income for identifying middle class. To my mind this is a better way. Because occupation is related with education and status. Several persons with high income may not be educated and may not occupy middle class status. But with occupation income is closely related.

The term elite is generally referred to group of persons who are respected and influential in society. In different sphere there might be different elite such as religious elite, social elite, political elite. As middle class in whatever way one defines is a class of educated professionals, hence many of the elite in society comes from this class. They are intellectuals and carry influence in social, political and cultural spheres.

In the developing countries the middle class both in the colonial and post- colonial period has emerged and expanded with the spread of higher education both in professional and humanistic spheres. With industrial growth service sector has expanded. This is what has happened in the post-colonial period in India.

This is also called tertiary sector of industry or service industry sector. Service sector provides services to the consumers which include financial institutions, trade, real estate, educational institutions, health care, legal assistance, tourism –transport and communication, hotels etc. Share of service sector in Indian economy in the last two decades is phenomenon. It is almost 49 per cent of India's GDP. It provides employment nearly 23 per cent of our labour force.

In my paper on Middle Class politics: A case of anti-reservation in Gujarat, published in 1987 in *EPW* I define middle class in relation with castes in Gujarat as follows: (In this article I have described historical growth of the middle class and castes in Gujarat)

> "The middle class is a class between labour and capital. It neither directly owns the means of production that pumps out the surplus generated by wage labour power nor does it, by its own labour, produce the surplus having use value and exchange value. Broadly speaking, this class consists of the petty-bourgeoise and the white-collar workers. The former are either self-employed or involved in the distribution of commodities and the latter are non-manual office workers, supervisors and professionals. Thus, in terms of occupations, shopkeepers, salesmen, brokers, government and non-government office-workers, writers and teachers, self-employed professionals such as engineers, pleaders, doctors, etc, constitute the middle class. Most of these occupations require at least some degree of formal education. This middle class is primarily a product of capitalist development as well as expansion of the functions of the state in the 19th and the 20th centuries. Though the petty bourgeoise and the managers did exist in precapitalist society, they constituted a tiny class. Industrial development and expansion of the market requires not only a larger managerial class than the earlier period but also impels the state to shoulder the responsibilities of monitoring market-competition and resolving the contradictions of capitalist development. Consequently, the state also requires a managerial class. Formal education contributes to the development of this class."

2

THE RISE OF MIDDLE CLASSES IN MODERN MANIPUR

Gangmumei Kamei

The emergence of the middle classes is an important phenomenon in the social history of a country. For the study of such a social problem, the knowledge of history, economics and sociology of the country is essential. Both historians and sociologists have studied the question of middle class by using their respective tools. A reference to the middle classes in a country implies the existence of several social classes, one above the middle class and another class below it. Karl Marx in his *The Communist Manifesto* declares that "the history of all hitherto existing society is the history of class struggles". Marx employs the term "class" to mean two major social groups which are divided into two big economic classes: the bourgeoisie and proletariat. Marx divides a society into two classes; the owner of the means of production and the other is the working class who work on the production. He uses the term bourgeoisie to mean the owners of mode of production and the proletariat to mean the working class. Max Weber, a German sociologist also mentions the existence of social classes into class stratification and stratification by prestige or social honour. In a more abstract sense the bourgeoisie is represented by the capital and the proletariat is represented by labour, a division of society into capitalist and working class. Marx mentions the existence of intermediary strata between the bourgeoisie and proletariat. This intermediary strata is the middle class whom Marx call petite bourgeoisie. However, it is extremely difficult to make a clear cut definition of a middle classes. The Marxian concept of social class is essentially an economic category between capital and the labour. Those who owns the means of production which employ others as workers for production are covered by these two terms the Capitalist and the Working Class. Between these two classes people who do not physically labour and involve in the material productions and who are involved in managing and exchanging the commodities in the market, who work as intellectuals are the petty bourgeoisie or the middle class. However for Max Weber, a social class and status are the basis of social stratification in which power and domination are important components to identify the differences. For him a social class is concerned with social status and power. Marx predicted that the intermediary strata would disappear but that has not happened yet.

The features of the middle classes are identified on the basis of occupation; they are professionals and white collar employees doing mostly non manual works. Another criteria to judge the middle class is on the basis of income. It is argued by some scholars that occupation and income are the identifying criteria of the middle classes. Again income is related with education and status. Persons with high income who are not educated will not be regarded as the middle class. Among the middle classes elite is a group of persons who are influential in the society. The elites who form the middle class are divided into religious elite, social elite and political elite. Usually a middle class is a class of educated professionals wherefrom come the elite. They are intellectuals who carry influence in social, political and cultural spheres. Service sector provides services to the consumers which include financial institution, trade, real estate, educational institutions, health care, legal assistance, transport and communication etc. In ancient Greece Aristotle observed in 306 B.C. that the citizens of the middle class were the best political community of a state.[1] The American writer Walt Whitman in 1858 described the middle class as the most valuable class in any community.[2]

In Indian context, B.B. Misra in his *The Indian Middle Classes: Their growth in modern times* (1961) classifies the Indian middle classes into four categories; the commercial middle class, the industrial middle class, the landed middle class and the educated middle class (learned professions). In this classification of B.B. Misra middle classes constitute the merchants and traders, the partisan and the skilled workers, the landed land owners and the learned professionals. B.B. Misra writes that the Indian middle class includes a body of merchants, agents and proprietors of modern trading firms; it also includes salaried executives such as managers, inspectors, supervisors and technical staff engaged in banking, trading and manufacturing businesses. It includes civil servants like the secretaries to the government, judges of the high courts, and officers who look after specialized services like agriculture, education, health etc. The educated professionals include lawyer and doctor, university and college teacher, writer and journalist, artist and musician, priest and religious preacher. Non manual workers include shop keeper and hotel keeper and group of clerks, assistants below the managerial and other professional levels. Middle classes also include the secondary school teacher and officer of the local bodies, social and political workers. According to Andre Beteille the emergence of the middle class was facilitated by modern education and consequent work opportunities available in offices set up for commercial, administration and other purposes by the colonial government.[3]

A question is raised whether middle classes existed in Indian history, ancient India, medieval India and modern India including British rule. B.B. Misra writes of pre-colonial Indian society. He writes, "Indian society in pre-British times consisted in the main of four elements: the king and his courtiers forming the bureaucratic apparatus of the state, the princely intellectuals comprising the scholarly and professional categories, the merchant called Vaishya and the agriculturalist including both artisans and peasants."[4] The general impression among the historians is that the middle classes did not grow up in India in a marked way. Reasons for this stunted growth of middle class were the prevalence of despotic form of government in India and the agricultural economy of the state. There was a low level of technological development and self sufficiency of the Indian villages. Indian society was indeed embedded in caste, religion and joint family system. Yet urban centres also grew up where a village was regarded as a place of pilgrimage, where a seat of provincial administration was located and where a trading centre grew up and where the artisan classes concentrated.

The Middle Classes in Ancient India

Sources of information indicate the prevalence of non manual occupations in ancient India like the priestly activities, the warfare, agricultural, industrial and trading. The priestly class consisted of teaching, Brahmin priest, astrologer, reciter of verses, physician, and priest presiding over sacrifices. Greek writer, Magasthenes refers to several castes of occupation. The last caste included counselors of the king and officials of the state, tribunal of justice and general administrators of public affairs. References are made to the various occupations, the religious denominations, trade guilds and schools of Vedic literatures.[5]

The Middle Classes in Medieval India

The Medieval Indian society consisted of two economically and politically dominant classes. One was the various rajas, chiefs and landlords who were hereditary feudal lords. They were popularly known as zamindars. Second was the revenue officers known as jagirdars. These two categories of hereditary officials lived largely on the social surplus produced by the peasants. Contemporary writers mentioned that there was no middle class. However there are references to the grant of lands to the officers in lieu of salary. These officers of different categories constituted the middle classes. There was a mention of the existence of traders, merchants and people involved in commercial activities. There was long distance caravan trade. There were many Indian money-lenders who acted as bankers. But every class in the society depended on agriculture including nobility, emerging middle class elements, peasants and workers. So the elements of middle class had already existed before the coming of the British.[6]

The Middle Classes in British Period

The British created the institution of middle class in India. It has been said that the middle class was a product of capitalist growth during the British period. The middle class which grew up during the British period were mostly non manual white collar workers like shop keepers, traders, merchants, business men, independent practitioners of professions and independent artisans. According to B.B. Misra by 1835 a middle class was in the process of formation. It consisted of owners of landed estates and urban properties, merchants, traders, members of various professions such as lawyers, doctors, journalists and writers which formed the members of the literary middle class. They were the products of the western education system. The aim of the British education policy was to produce persons influenced by western ideas to follow western way of life and thought, a group of men who were Indian by blood but Englishmen in thought. By the end of the 19th century, a middle class of a general vision had emerged in India. B.B. Misra again writes, "a great middle class with a general vision, a competent leadership and a body of social ideas had come into existence. Liberalism was their creed: self government and economic freedom, their political objective, the regeneration of India organized as a progressive forward looking community, accepting freely from the west its science, and its new learning was the great ideal they place before themselves."[7]

Middle Classes in Pre-colonial Manipur

We are confronted with the question whether the middle classes existed in the pre-colonial Manipur. She was a monarchy in which the government led by the king and the peasants who constituted the subjects existed. The monarchy with its feudalistic paraphernalia constituted the political class. The subjects of Manipur, under the feudal system of Lallup bore the brunt of service as a soldier or a peace time construction workers rendered feudal service to the king. There was no much scope for other professions for example merchants and traders. Trade and commerce existed but these were part time professions. So before the conquest of Manipur by the British in 1891, the economy was controlled by the state. Therefore there was no much scope of rise of a middle class between the king and the subjects though there was scope for feudal lords who helped the king in the administration of the kingdom. Only when the British introduced their administrative, political, economic and social policy for about half a century, middle classes emerged in Manipur.

Middle Classes in Colonial Period

Middle class in Manipur was a phenomenon of colonialism. The following are the features of middle class in the kingdom.

(i) The introduction of English education produced a lower level of educated persons.

(ii) Government employment to educated class as sepoy or police, teachers, petty government servants in revenue, education, medical and public works. The police and education departments provided jobs for persons who were educated up to primary levels.

(iii) The political class which was formed of the members of the former nobility related to the royal family who were educated became the members of the Manipur State Durbar appointed by the Maharaja. The members of the Manipur State Durbar who were *de facto* ministers of the state helped the Maharaja in the administration of the valley of Manipur constituted the political class.

(iv) Literary class consisted of those who were educated up to the secondary levels in the local high schools. They were given scholarships and stipends by the state. Those who passed matriculation level were sent out for higher education in the colleges in Assam and Bengal, particularly Gauhati, Sylhet, Dacca and Calcutta. This group formed the literary middle class. They became school teachers, writers, journalists and government servants. They formed a very powerful middle class during the last decade of Maharaja Churachand's rule.

(v) Mercantile class: The British followed a free trade policy towards Manipur. They encouraged imports in Manipur mostly consumer goods. They encouraged export of rice of Manipur to outside the state to supply to the armed forces stations. The export of rice was monopolized by contractors. The local traders did not have opportunities to be involved in export trade. They gave permission to "foreign traders" like Marwaris who carried on monopoly in this trade. Trade and commerce were in the hands of the outside merchants. Only during the Second World War and after, merchants and businessmen including contractors of public works grew up in Manipur.

(vi) Educated middle class. The British government encouraged the establishment of primary schools in the early period of their rule. The Christian missionaries established schools and hospitals for tribal areas along with their conversion into Christianity. Maharaja Churachand Singh was a patron of modern education. There was only a high school named Johnstone High School with facilities for reading up to Class X. This school was affiliated to Calcutta University in 1924. A few more high schools were established in the name of the Maharaja and his daughters: Churachand High School, Tamphasana Girls High School and Tombisana High School. The Christian mission schools taught a large number of tribals up to the primary level. Some were sent outside Manipur. So this educated middle class took up many social reforms for the state. They entered in to the services of the government and influenced the policy of the state.

(vii) Manipur was an agrarian state. Though artisans were available, industries did not grow due to absence of capitalists. Due to the absence of industries both the owner of the means of production and the workers were absent. No bourgeoisie and no proletariat.

During the period of the direct British management of Manipur (1891-1907), the British introduced Indian pattern of administration; revenue, education, public works and police; and they gave importance to the education activities in the state. For running the administration the British authorities imported government employees from the province of Assam to become school teachers, petty officials of the revenue department for survey and settlement works. Because of the reluctance of the youth of Manipur to join the state police, recruitment to this force was open to outsiders. Those who passed out of the schools run by the government and the Christian missions were employed in hill administration, revenue administration, education and police, lambus, chowkidars, peons, road muhorrirs and interpreters. Among the educated persons of Manipur of the time the name of Haodeijamba Chaitanya Singh attracted the attention of the government and public. He was, to use a modern term, a social activist during the period before the World War I. His father was Haodeijam Gokul Singh, an employee of the Chief Commissioner of Assam. He was born in Shillong in 1867. He had early education in a mission school. He grew up in the cosmopolitan atmosphere of Shillong. He was conversant with Bengali, English, Hindustani and Manipuri, his mother tongue. He was among the few Manipuris who got opportunity of a new English education and upbringing in an urban area of Assam. After 15 years of service in Assam government, his father returned to Imphal and after the Anglo-Manipur War of 1891 Chaitanya was employed as a postal overseer along the Cachar-Manipur road. Later on he joined the státe office of the British authority as a Tehsildar clerk in 1895.[8]

Chaitanya was fully aware of the changes brought about by the British rule in the country. He devoted to writing of five literary works given below.

1. *Manipurer Itihas* printed at the Baptist Mission, Sylhet and published by the Political Agent of Manipur (not dated) but it was presumably published in 1890.
2. *Khamba Thoibigi Warini* (1899) dealing with the romantic story of Khamba and Thoibi of Moirang
3. *Khahi Ngamba* (1900) dealing with the rule of Maharaja Gambhir Singh who defeated the Khasi rebels.
4. *Takhel Ngamba* (1902). This was a history of Garibniwaz who defeated the Tripuris in early 18th century.
5. *Chingthangkhomba* (1902). It is a history of Maharaja Bhagyachandra.

Apart from his publication of history and some literary works Haodeijamba Chaitanya was involved in making protest against the oppressive rule of the Maharaja of Manipur. In 1892 Major Maxwell, the Political Agent and the Superintendent of the state of Manipur declared the abolition of slavery and feudal service known as Lallup. These had removed the burden from the common people but the Maharaja or his nobles tried to continue this practice. Chaitanya on his own initiative made complaints against these practices to the Political Agent who approved of his protest movement. However a scandal occurred in Manipur on account of an affair of Major Maxwell with Rajkumari Sanatombi, a Manipuri princess and a daughter of former Maharaja Sur Chandra Singh. This princess was already married to one Nongmaithem Manik

Chand Singh, a small trader. During his frequent absence due to travel outside Manipur, the Political Agent and the princess came to know each other. Her husband Manik Chand came to know of this affair and rebuked his wife for this. Rajkumari Sanatombi eloped with the Political Agent and stayed in the official residence of the Political Agent as his concubine. Nongmaithem Manik Chand was really unhappy over this behaviour of his wife and he took the help of Chaitanya to write letters against the Political Agent. Maxwell suspected Chaitanya of his hand in this complaint. Major Maxwell removed Chaitanya from service and in 1900 he was exiled from Manipur. Haodeijamba Chaitanya submitted an appeal petition against the behaviour of Major Maxwell to the Governor General of India. In 1905 Chaitanya was given a reprieve by the Governor General and he was reinstated in the service of Manipur government.

Chaitanya was against the practice of forced labour imposed by British on the rural people. This practice was known as Pothang system. There was an agitation in Thoubal area against this practice. He supported the movement for the abolition of the forced labour. The Political Agent, Col. Cole discovered the involvement of Haodeijamba Chaitanya in this movement. He was removed from the service and was vanished from Manipur. He made several appeals for his return to Manipur and a grant of pension which were rejected by the British government. He spent his last days in Cachar in poverty. Hoadeijamba Chaitanya was an educated man, a writer and a social leader for the upliftment of the cause of the common people. He was the first man, who raised his pen against the British authorities and suffered from it.

A political event of early British rule was the installation of Raja Churachand Singh as the ruler of Manipur in 1907. The "Rules for the Management of the State of Manipur" provided for the constitution of a state durbar to help the Raja in the administration of valley areas of Manipur. The members of the first Manipur State Durbar included Rajkumar Dumbra Singh, the eldest brother of the Raja, Pandit Bindu Madhop Shastri, an intelligent and widely traveled Brahmin, the father of future leader of Manipur Lalit Madhop Sharma, M. Tamra Singh, a Major in the native army of Manipur, Sougaijam Ibungochouba Singh, son of General Balaram, a minister of Maharaja Chandrakirti Singh and a father of first law graduate of Manipur, Sougaijam Samarendra Singh, N. Yaiskulakpa and N. Gokul Singh. These members belonged to the influential background[9]. The members of the Manipur State Durbar were a mixture of nobility and common men. They constituted the political class in the colonial Manipur.

During the World War I, Manipur gave assistance to the British government in their war against Germany. Manipur gave a double company of Manipuri soldiers consisting of 250 men for service in Mesopotamia (now Iraq). A labour corps of 2000 tribesmen was sent to France. They were led by the British officers, but the educated tribals were appointed as the interpreters. After the War, they were taken to London and introduced to King Emperor George V in Buckingham Palace. This exposure broadened the mindset of the tribal people whose leaders were educated in mission schools and employed in the hill administration under the British. But it was after the end of the First World War that the middle classes grew up in Manipur in a rudimentary form. Education was encouraged and the educated middle classes like the lawyers, doctors, writers and journalists, teachers and government servants grew up. Among the lawyers, mention may be made of S. Samarendra Singh and Laimayum Iboongohal Singh. S. Samarendra Singh was from Calcutta University and became a member of the Manipur State Durbar several times. He participated in political life of Manipur in the least years of colonial rule in Manipur and in independent India. L. Iboongohal Singh was member of Manipur judiciary and a scholar. He was an intimate advisor of the Maharaja Sir Churachand Singh. Among the medical practitioners, Dr. N. Govardhan Singh, Dr. N. Leiren Singh and Dr. L. Kamal were the pioneers. Among the scholars the names of Sinam Krishnamohan Singh, the first post graduate degree holder with law and Dwijamani Deb Sharma, an M.A. in Sanskrit may be mentioned. Manipur produced literary men in the person of Kh. Chaoba, a poet and a novelist, L. Kamal, a poet and novelist, Hijam Anganghal Singh, a poet and novelist, Arambam Dorendra Singh, a poet, novelist and playwright. They lived in the period between 1920 and 1950. Among these groups a person who was a versatile man was Hijam Irabot Singh. He was educated in Dacca, the first editor of a Manipuri journal, a sportsman, actor and an essayist. He was also a political leader. He can be said to be a representative of his age. He started his career as a school teacher; after marriage with a princess of Maharaja Churachand Singh's family, he was appointed a judge of the Sadar Panchayat Court. He founded the first political party of Manipur known as Nikhil Hindu Manipuri Mahasabha (1934). He was involved in the second women agitation of 1939-40 and was jailed for three years. He became a member of the Communist Party of India while in jail in Sylhet. After the Second World War he was involved in the political affairs of the state. He founded the Manipur Krishak Sabha. He also organized the Communist revolution in the state.

We may mention the educational background of the members of the Manipur State Durbar appointed by the Maharaja. S. Samarendra Singh, a graduate from Rippon College from Calcutta, M.K. Priya Brata Singh, a graduate from Allahabad University, L. Iboongohal Singh a law graduate of Calcutta University, S. Nodiachand Singh a graduate from Presidency College, Calcutta, W. Yumjao Singh an archaeologist and a historian from Government College, Dacca, W. Chaoba Singh a graduate from Calcutta University, M. Radhamohan Singh a law graduate from Calcutta University and A. Ibotomcha Singh from M.C. College of Dacca University were members of the State Durbar between 1920 and 1947[10]. Except Maharajkumar Priya Brata Singh others belonged to the educated middle classes of the colonial period.

Contemporaneous to the middle classes of the valley areas, the hill areas also produced several graduates who participated in the political affairs and administration of the state of Manipur. We have some distinguished and educated young leaders from the hills in the last decade of the British rule. We may mention R. Khathing of Ukhrul who after graduation joined the British Indian Army, participated in the Second World War, and ended up as a Major. He became a Hill minister in the government of Maharajkumar Priya Brata Singh in the Interim period. A. Daiho a graduate of Gauhati of 1938 batch became a prosperous businessman and contractor during the Second World War, was appointed a member of the Manipur State Constitution Making

Body. He organized a political agitation in north Manipur under the banner of Naga National League. He was jailed and released after Manipur was merged with India. He was made a member of the Advisory Council and he was elected to Manipur Territorial Assembly and became a Finance Minister. Thongkhopao Kipgen was a brilliant student of Cotton College, Gauhati and joined the government service. Later on he became a Secretary of Government of Manipur and was promoted to IAS. He retired as a Chief Secretary of Goa. T.C. Tiankham was elected to Manipur Legislative Assembly in 1948 and became Speaker of the Assembly. After the dissolution of the Assembly as a result of merger of Manipur with the Indian Union, he joined the services and became an IAS. Another remarkable man was Teba Kilong who was a minister under Chief Minister M.K. Priya Brata Singh. It has been stated that the middle class consciousness in the colonial period took its form in the period from 1920 to 1940.[11]

The election of 1948 threw up a number of educated persons as the members of the Manipur Legislative Assembly. Most of the members of the Assembly of 1948 belonged to the middle classes. Some of them continued to participate in the political affairs of Manipur even after the merger. They continued to constitute what is known as the political class of Manipur. It is worth mentioning that the leaders of Manipur State Congress like Sinam Krishnamohan Singh, L. Jugeswar Singh, Lalit Madhop Sharma, R.K. Bhubon Singh, and S. Indramani Singh were an urban educated lot. They belonged to the educated middle class of Manipur. We have already mentioned the political role of Hijam Irabot Singh as a reformer, a political agitator, a revolutionary. He was surrounded by a large number of youth leaders namely M. Meghachandra Singh, a post graduate of Calcutta University, N. Binoy Singh of Cotton College Gauhati, Ng. Mohendro, a youth leader of Imphal and Th. Boro Singh who constituted young Turk section of Communist movement in Manipur. These leaders continued to play in the political life of Manipur. M. Meghachandra Singh became a minister of Manipur and a Member of Parliament and Ng. Mohendro became a Member of Parliament. N. Binoy Singh was a youth leader of the Communist party. He was actively involved in the Communist Revolution of 1950-51. He was jailed for involvement in the Manipur Conspiracy case of 1952. After

CPI became a constitutional party he could not take part in the role of the leadership but he continued to be involved in the social activism till the beginning of the 21st century.

The youth leaders who belonged to the Congress and Socialist schools of thought were brilliant students of Calcutta University. H. Ranbir Singh an M.A. from Presidency College of Calcutta was a leader of the Congress led Chhatra Parishad. L. Achou Singh was the leader of the Socialist Congress and was involved in the affairs of the Manipur State Congress. Later on he carved out a role for himself in the Socialist movement in the country.

We cannot but remember the role of educationists in the colonial period. One was Dwijamani Deb Sharma who served in the Education Department of the Government of Manipur. He retired after 15 years and devoted himself for establishment of a degree college in Manipur. He became a Principal of D.M. College at Imphal. After merger he continued to be involved in the politics of Manipur. He was elected the first Chairman in the Manipur Territorial Council (1957-58). He continued to contribute in the establishment of colleges in Manipur. He donated the Ghana Priya Women College (G.P. Women College) in 1964. He also donated several music and performing art colleges. An educationist of repute in the colonial period was Konjengbam Gouro Singh who was the Head Master of Johnstone High School for many years. He became an Education Minister under the Constitutional Monarchy of Manipur in 1948-49. Chingakham Pishak Singh a well known educationist and a product of Calcutta University sacrificed his career in public life when he had to resign from the General Secretaryship of Nikhil Manipuri Mahasabha when he was advised not to give up his teaching profession. He became a member of the Manipur Assembly from the constituency of Education. Later on he became the Head Master of Churachand High School and Principal of erstwhile Manipur College, a premier private college of Imphal.

A man who started his career as a government servant but was endowed with scholarship in the field of Manipuri literature was Asangbam Mineketan Singh. He became a learned teacher of Manipuri in D.M. College and Jawaharlal Nehru University Centre at Imphal. R.K. Shitaljit Singh was an educationist devoted to his profession. He was a writer and a novelist. He became a Head Master of Ram Lal Paul High School and devoted to study of Sanskrit literature specially the Gita. His contribution to education, Sanskrit and Manipuri literature was really great.

Among the educated tribal middle classes of Manipur, we should remember the former students of Rev. William Pettigrew of American Baptist Mission in Manipur. His students who contributed to the religious and public life of Manipur were M.K. Shimray who was an MLA in 1948 and became President of the Tangkhul Long, T. Luikham was a scholar and a missionary from Ukhrul who wrote scholarly works on Tangkhul culture and the famous Silver Jubilee report of Tangkhul Baptist in 1948, Teba Kilong who was a prolific writer in tribal dialects and was as mentioned above a minister under M.K. Priya Brata Singh, Longkhovel Kom etc. Among the public leaders who became member of the Assembly and later on Member of Parliament was R. Suisa of Somdal, Ukhrul. Thus at the time of merger of Manipur, an incipient middle class had emerged in Manipur among the tribals.

Middle Classes in Post-Colonial Period

Manipur was a princely state under the British paramountcy for 56 years (1891-1947). Manipur continued to be an agrarian country; trade and commerce did not develop in a fast rate except during the post-Second World War period. Industry did not develop; however artisans were carrying on handicrafts mostly textiles and basketry. We have seen that the educated middle classes had grown up during the colonial period. Education had grown up; in the tribal areas. Christianity had opened up the mindset of the people through the expanding activities of the state and Christian missions. Thus during the post-colonial period which covered the second half of 20th century and beyond, the features of middle classes had emerged. In the absence of industrial development agrarian economy confined the people to agriculture but the planned development activities of the Government of India had led to the growth of capitalist economy. Manipur has come to possess all the elements of the capitalist economy as the colonial economy of the British has been transformed into the capitalist economy of India. Colonial rule had left behind a semblance of educated middle classes which manned the expanding horizon of the state.

As explained on the features of the middle classes, they were conditioned by factors of occupation, income and education. This occupation consists of the professions of the educated classes namely legal profession, medical profession, engineering profession, government service, trade and business and teaching and writing profession. Therefore we specify the members of the occupations as lawyers, doctors, engineers, government officials, writers and teachers.

Legal Profession

The Indian pattern of administration had to deal with many laws and regulations. The British had introduced the complex Indian laws connected with crime and punishment, police, revenue and land settlement, taxation laws and others. The complexity of law was not easily understood by the common people. Therefore the help of the lawyers or experts who understood legal process was utilized at different levels of administration and courts. During the colonial period the services of the lawyers were not much abundant but with the merger of Manipur in the Indian Union in 1949, the central government introduced various laws, the young men of the valley studied law in various universities and colleges of India. A law graduate was respected. With the establishment of many courts ranging from the court of the Chief Commissioner to that of Judicial Commissioner, session courts and subordinate court of the SDOs a large number of advocates were utilized. In the beginning, Manipur state employed mostly Bengali pleaders in Manipur. A number of young men had become law graduates. They were mostly from Calcutta University, Allahabad University and Bombay University. During the pre-statehood days the number of advocates was few. The higher levels of legal profession consisted of a few well educated law graduates. Prominent among them in the early period were N. Ibotombi Singh an advocate who became a Judge of Gauhati High Court later on. The second group consisted of Yendrembam Imo Singh, R.K. Manisana Singh and Takyeljam Bhuban Singh. They were the pioneer advocates. While Y. Imo Singh and T. Bhuban Singh became Advocate General of the state. R.K. Manisana Singh became Chief Justice of Gauhati High Court. A prominent advocate of Allahabad University was Ahanthem

Nilamani Singh who was a patriarch of the lawyers of Manipur. With the establishment of LMS Law College, legal education was open to a large number of students and government employees. The products of this college became members of the legal profession. Many of them became members of the Bench from the highest to the lowest. It was found that legal knowledge is essential for the administration of the state and it has become quite popular in Manipur.

The Manipur Bar Association which consists of all the lawyers of the state became a very active body for the moral supervision of the law officers of the state. They gave opinion on legal and constitutional issues of the state. Members of the Bar are found acting in a responsible way. Legal profession is popular among the Meitei educated youths. Among the tribal, legal profession is not very popular. However in the post-statehood period many tribal lawyers are produced. A pioneer was Major P.C. Misao who was an army lawyer in his service days. Major Misao opened up the profession to tribal youths while several Meitei lawyers had become Judges of the High Court. A few tribal lawyers could come up to that level. However two lawyers of Manipur tribals who served in neighbouring states had become Government Advocates and Judges of the High Court. Justice W.A. Shishak an Advocate General of Nagaland State was appointed a Judge of the Gauhati High Court. Later on he became Chief Justice of High Court of Himachal Pradesh and Chattishgarh. After retirement he was made Chairman of the Manipur Human Rights Commission. Justice Vaiphei also entered the services of the Mizoram Government and from there he was appointed as a Judge of Gauhati High Court. Of the lawyers who joined electoral politics of Manipur, we may mention three leaders who became Chief Ministers of the state. They were R.K. Dorendra Singh, Rajkumar Jaichandra Singh and Radhabinod Koijam.

Several senior advocates from Manipur were appointed as judges of Gauhati High Court but none so far had joined the Supreme Court. Legal profession for the talented lawyers was lucrative and popular. However it had become highly competitive in Manipur. Women lawyers had also increased their number. Some of them became judges at different levels of judiciary.

Lawyers continue to play an important role in the civil life of Manipur.

Writers among the lawyers had written on the constitution of India and Judicial system of the state dealing with specific laws current in Manipur. The teachers of the Law College wrote on legal issues as per their curriculum. A special mention may be made of R.K. Manisana Singh's *The Judicial History of Manipur* and M. Ibohal Singh's *Constitution of India* which are very scholarly and perceptive analysis of the law.

Medical Profession

Dr. R. Brown was the first medical practitioner with a degree of F.R.C.S. who came to Manipur as a Political Agent during the time of Maharaja Chandrakirti Singh. During the colonial period several surgeons had served in Manipur. The post of the civil surgeon was an important post in the colonial administration of Manipur. With the coming of central rule in Manipur, medical department was expanded from a General Civil Hospital at Imphal to a large number of primary health centers, community health centers, district hospitals and two medical colleges. During the colonial period the diploma holding medical practitioners having a diploma of L.M.P. whose holders were called doctors in general. During the Second World War many doctors and nurses had come to Manipur to treat the dead and the wounded during the war. After merger with India a number of brilliant students from Manipur underwent medical studies. They were products of medical colleges of Calcutta and Dibrugarh.

The pioneer doctors were Dr. Ph. Tonsana Singh and Dr. Satyabati Devi the first woman doctor. With the encouragement given by the government of India several doctors underwent training in foreign countries especially United Kingdom. Mention may be made of Dr. N.B. Roy who got FRCS from Edinburgh, Dr. Th. Jugindra Singh who got MRCP from Edinburgh and Dr. P. Kumud Singh, an MRCP from London. With the introduction of M.S. Degree in India the number of doctors trained in MRCP and FRCS has gone down. Every year the government selected students for study in MBBS/BDS in the medical colleges selected for them by Government of India. There were doctors who are trained in M.D. and M.S. Several doctors got research degree like D.M. The medical education got a great boost with the establishment of Regional Medical College (RMC) at Imphal in 1964. This college was converted as Regional Institute of Medical Sciences sponsored by Government of India. This institute had produced a large number of medical graduates and post graduates. The government is also running a Nursing College which produces trained nurses for service in the hospitals of Manipur. Recently the Government of Manipur had founded a new medical college named Jawaharlal Nehru Institute of Medical Sciences (JNIMS) at Imphal. This second college would go a long way in meeting the needs of the medical students for undergoing training.

There grew up a number of private medical hospitals and research centers at Imphal city. Specialist services were made available to these private hospitals as many of the doctors from the medical colleges are employed in the private hospitals as part time doctors. Prominent among the private hospitals and clinics are Chamber of Commerce Medical and Research Centre, Shija Hospital, Imphal Hospital etc. There are specialized clinics for maternity and gynecology. Pathological diagnostic centers are also available. With these hospitals and clinics Imphal has become a centre for medical treatment from neighbouring states. Moreover the cost of medical treatment is comparatively cheaper in Imphal.

Manipur government employs a large number of doctors of different levels, medical officers, physicians, surgeons, specialists like neurology, radiology, orthopedics etc. The medical department use to post these doctors throughout Manipur including interior and hill areas but these doctors are not easily available in their hospitals where they are posted.

Medical profession has always attracted a large number of students both male and female. They got employment both in the government hospitals and private hospitals. Despite the increasing number of doctors the demand for doctors in the villages is still increasing. The medical degree is the first choice for most of the talented young students of Manipur. Their parents do not hesitate to invest in the education of the doctors. The doctors constitute an important segment of the educated middle classes in Manipur. We find a differentiation between the tribals and non tribals in this profession. While the medical studies for the valley people is quite abundant there is comparatively smaller number among the tribal people of Manipur. The availability of seats in the medical colleges has been facilitated by reservation for the Scheduled Tribe and Scheduled Caste. Well to do and not so well to do parents can afford the cost of medical studies for the tribal students also. Now a sizeable number of tribal doctors had come out including specialized doctors. A tribal doctor with specialization in Forensic Science became Director of the prestigious Regional Institute of Medical Sciences at Imphal. However number of medical practitioners among the tribes is still small.

Regarding the high level of knowledge and efficiency among the doctors belonging to Meitei community, it has been suggested that the Meiteis from the early times had a tradition of practice of herbal medicines. Perhaps this cultural factor was a valid reason for the growth and emergence of modern medical science among them. There is also non allopathic medical science practiced among the people of Manipur. The tribal physicians still widely use traditional herbal medicine for treatment of the sick in the hill areas. There are doctors who are trained in Ayurvedic, Homeopathic and Unani medicines. They are quite popular among the users of these medicines. Medical profession and the doctors had a bright future. And it is expected that the doctors of Manipur would play a great role in the medical world of India.

The Civil Services

The merger of Manipur into the Indian Union brought a progressive change in the administration of Manipur state. The higher British bureaucracy during the colonial period was appointed from the Indian Civil Service (ICS), Indian Political Service and specialized doctors and engineers who headed the Medical Department and PWD. The middle level civil service was recruited from the provincial Assam civil Services. Lower level civil services like the police, revenue, judiciary and education were recruited from the educated intelligentsia among the urban middle class of Manipur. With the abolition of monarchy, the administration of the state was taken over by higher bureaucracy of the Indian administration. The monarch and his council of ministers were replaced by the members of the upper Indian bureaucracy. Manipur was under a central administration from

1949 to 1972. The Chief Commissioner was the head of the administration. And the Chief Commissioners were appointed from amongst the ICS and IAS. Manipur was a one district Union Territory with a small secretariat. However the middle and lower secretariat services were appointed from the local civil servants. The officials and petty government employees of the princely state of Manipur were absorbed into the services of the Union Territory. But officials of the princely state who qualified for the gazetted rank were few. Some of the officers of the princely state were absorbed as under secretary, EAC, SDC etc. The teachers and the police who belonged to both civil and armed sectors were absorbed in the service of the new administration. Thus the new administration had become a purely Indian administration. Instead of the Maharaja and the British Political Agent, there was the Chief Commissioner often a member of the ICS in the early phase and of the IAS in the later phase. The Deputy Commissioner who was the district magistrate of Manipur became the most important official of the Union Territory. The middle officers were sub divisional officers and sub deputy collectors who manned administration.

After the merger, the Chief Court of Manipur was abolished and the Chief Commissioner had assumed the head of the judicial services. The government of India appointed later on a Judicial Commissioner to be the head of judiciary. There was no much separation of executive and judiciary in the powers of the officers both at the middle and lower level of administration.

There was none who could qualify for IAS or IPS from amongst the local people of Manipur. Some of them could get promotion to IAS. Mention may be made of few brilliant officers of the state. Major R. Khathing who was a Hill Minister during 1949 returned to Government service and entered the Indian Frontier Administrative Services in erstwhile NEFA. He later on joined the services of Nagaland and promoted to IAS and became its Chief Secretary. Later on he was sent as India's Ambassador to Burma (Myanmar). One brilliant officer Thongkhopao Kipgen who also joined the Union Territory administration as an Under Secretary got promotion to IAS and became the Chief Secretary of Goa. Sanasam Gourahari Singh who was private secretary to the Maharaja was absorbed in the new administration and was promoted to IAS. He became a Secretary to the Government of Manipur. Hawaibam Ranbir Singh who started his career as a lecturer in the government D.M. College was absorbed in the new administration. He was promoted to IAS and became education secretary and was in charge of newly established Manipur University as its Acting Vice-Chancellor for some period. W. Shaiza of Ukhrul was absorbed in the IAS and he became Chief Secretary of Union Territory of Delhi.

Manipur became a full fledged state in 1972. After this the government of Manipur recruited the first batch of Manipur Civil Service (MCS) and Manipur Police Service (MPS) through a public examination conducted by Manipur Public Service Commission. Earlier the Union Public Service Commission conducted examination for MCS and MPS and a few candidates from Manipur were selected. The examination conducted by MPSC selected direct recruits to MCS and MPS mostly from the candidates of Manipur state. This first batch of directly recruited civil service men consisted of brilliant young men from different universities. Whenever there were vacancies, the Public Service Commission conducted examination for recruitment. The first and second batches of officers were regarded to be very efficient. Most of them were promoted to IAS and IPS. These young officers became the steel frame of administration of Manipur state. Manipur could claim to have a civil service consisting of her own officers. Of course Manipur continues to have its cadre of IAS directly recruited from Union Public Service Commission but so far no one from the MCS cadre has been made as the Chief Secretary of Manipur. Police officers belonging to MPS were promoted to IPS and became officers of the Police Department. At least three members of the IPS from Manipur were appointed Director General of Police in the state. The MCS/IAS became Deputy Commissioners and Secretaries of the state. The MPS/IPS became Superintendent of Police in the districts and Commandant of the Armed Police called the Manipur Rifles and the India Reserve Battalion. Recently members of the Manipur Finance Service (MFS) and Manipur Secretariat Service (MSS) were recruited through the Manipur Public Service Commission. And the eligible officers were promoted to All India Cadre. The officers of these cadres were recruited or promoted from amongst the officers of the state. Now the civil service mostly consisted of indigenous officers of the state.

Some bright young men and women were also recruited for the Indian Foreign Service (IFS). Major R. Khathing we have stated became an Ambassador. Two IFS officers namely, L. Keivom and S. Kipgen became Ambassadors. Keivom became a High Commissioner to New Zealand and S. Kipgen became an Ambassador to Ukraine. E. Sanamani Singh started his career as a lecturer of a college. He joined the civil services and was promoted to IAS. He became a distinguished poet and was a winner of Sahitya Academi Award for Manipuri literature.

At one time it was found that the Scheduled Tribes succeeded in getting the IAS and IPS through the UPSC. Kapani Mao was the first IAS recruited from Manipur through the UPSC. He joined the Madhya Pradesh Cadre. He was followed by H. Jelshyam who became the Chief Secretary of Manipur. Others were K. Kipgen, P.L. Thanga, Ameisingh Luikham, R. Muivah, Christinia Raikhan etc. The first among the Meitei young men to have come out successful in IAS examination was Rajkumar Phalguni. He ended up as a Secretary of the Ministry of DONER and North Eastern Council. R.K. Dinesh was another IAS officer. A Muslim young man succeeded in becoming a member of the Indian Foreign Service (IFS). Another All India Service with the rank of IAS is the Indian Forest Service. Brilliant students from Manipur succeeded to become IFS directly or on promotion. There are other All India Services of the A and B Groups like Indian Revenue Service, Indian Railway Service, Indian Postal Service, Indian Account and Audit Service and Indian Defence Account Service in which the young men and women from Manipur were recruited. A brief glance of these officers shows that every community of Manipur is now represented in the All India and State Civil Services. Some officers belonging to the IAS and IAAS joined politics and became ministers of the state. They were E. Kunjeshor Singh, IAS and C. Doungel, IAAS. Both of them became Finance ministers. An officer became a Chief Minister of the state. He was Yangmaso Shaiza who also became an M.P.

The Defence Services including the Army and Air force recruited officers from Manipur both through the regular and emergency services. They were trained in the military colleges of India. Well known names among the old military officers were Captain Maharajkumar P.B. Singh, Captain M.K. Jai Singh,

Major R. Khathing, M.C., Major Rajkumar Madhurjyajit Singh, Lt. Col. H. Bhuban Singh. There are younger officers who were the products of military colleges. Some of them had become Colonels, Brigadiers and Major General. There are a large number of young men both tribal and non tribal in the armed forces of the country. They also joined the paramilitary forces like the CRPF, BSF, Assam Rifles, CISF and Indo-Tibetan Police Force. The officers and men of the armed forces bring both lucrative income and prestige for the state.

Engineering Profession

During the colonial period the office of the state engineer mostly a British engineer was entrusted with the work of the PWD. During the Second World War the roads and bridges, electricity and water supply were expanded. Therefore the Assam PWD consisting of Assam's engineers headed by one executive engineer looked after the highways from Dimapur to Moreh. Other roads were looked after by Manipur Works Department. After merger, PWD headed by an officer of the rank of executive engineer looked after the construction works of the government buildings, roads and bridges, electricity and water supply. When Manipur was made a Union Territory the PWD was looked after by an officer entitled Principal Engineering Officer. When Manipur became a state, the PWD was diversified into four separate departments under one Chief Engineer each; PWD, Electricity, Irrigation and Flood Control, Public Health and Water Supply. Many engineers were employed in these departments. During the Union Territory days the engineering officers were recruited by the UPSC or central government on deputation. Outside engineers were employed. However many brilliant young students from Manipur who were trained in engineering colleges of Calcutta and later on Assam Engineering College were recruited to the lower level of the Engineering Services. Late Yambem Tombi Singh was the first engineering graduate of Manipur. He became Principal Engineering Officer and Chief Engineer later on. There grew up a number of engineers who became Assistant Engineers, Executive Engineers, Superintending Engineers and even Chief Engineers. The name of Brajamani Mukherjee an engineering graduate from Manipur was trained in United States of America for his M.Tech degree. He became later on a Chief Engineer of PWD, Manipur. Other engineers with specialization in their respective fields like electricity, pubic health, irrigation and flood control were also produced. Engineering profession was very popular because of its lucrative incomes. Many young men aspired for becoming an engineer which was coterminous with becoming rich. A new branch of engineering profession was the architecture whose need was felt by the government and the people who plan to construct big and beautiful buildings. Architecture has become a popular branch of housing engineering. As the activities of the state have expanded in different fields, the services of the engineers are needed. But a small state like Manipur cannot employ all the trained engineers in the services of the state. These engineers join the private services of the contractors and construction firms who take up big construction projects in the state and outside. The latest addition to the expansion of the engineering profession is the growth of electronics and computer science. Large numbers of computer engineers have been trained in the engineering colleges. Some of them are employed in the state services and many of them had been employed in the corporate sector of industry. Electronics and Computer science are attracting the attention of many prospective learners.

Writers and Journalists

The educated middle class consists of teachers, writers and journalists. In the colonial period the middle class was composed of the teachers of the schools who became writers and journalists. In the post-colonial period education had expanded enormously. In 1946 there was a college named D.M. College with 46 students. After merger a number of private colleges grew up, Imphal College and Manipur College were premier private colleges. After statehood a large number of colleges including Law College and B.Ed College were sprung up all over the state. Every district has a Government college and the earlier private colleges were taken over by the state. In 1980 a University was established. Government of India also established one Agriculture College known as Central Agriculture University (CAU). A regional campus of the Indira Gandhi National Tribal University was established at Imphal. There are also a large number of higher secondary schools and high schools. The primary schools are found almost in every locality of the valley and the hills.

These educational institutions ranging from primary schools to the university require a large number of teachers. During the colonial period there were many primary schools and few high schools. In the post colonial period a large number of teachers were recruited for the different levels of schools ranging from junior basic schools to high schools. For primary schools even non matriculates were appointed as teachers. For the higher classes matriculates to graduates were appointed as teachers. The high schools required trained graduates and in service trainings were given to teachers for the courses of B.T./B.Ed. The education department provided the largest number of employment of which teachers constituted a high percentage of the employees. Therefore teaching gave largest employment to the educated. In the early period, the school teachers became writers of text books prescribed by the state. They also wrote many literary works, poetry, novel, prose, dramas and essays. The bulk of literary works was produced by the teachers.

The university and colleges require teachers of different grades; lecturer, senior lecturer, reader and professor. They require higher qualifications like post graduates with higher research degrees. The University Grants Commission prescribes the qualification for recruitment of college and university teachers. In the early stage of college education for example for recruitment to government D.M. College, it was the Union Public Service Commission which recruited the lecturers and senior lecturers for this college. For the private colleges, the governing bodies appointed the teachers but most of them did not pay the UGC scale of pay to the college teachers. However, because of the availability of qualified teachers there was no dearth of teachers for the private colleges. After the large scale conversion of private colleges to government colleges the state government met the expenditure of paying the teachers. The problem of private colleges still remains. The teachers of the colleges wrote books ranging form creative literary works to different discipline of study like social science, history, life sciences, mathematics and natural sciences. Thess college and the university teachers constitute the intellectuals segment of the educated middle class. The scholars of the university had written on scholarly works based on original researches. The Manipur University produced a large number of learned books on different disciplines. The Central Agriculture University had produced several research works on agricultural sciences. Manipur now possesses a community of learned scholars and intellectuals. There has been great progress in literary production of the writers. The nature of the creative works produced during this period include poetry, novel, prose, drama, criticism, linguistics, biography and travelogue, folk literature and narratives. Some teachers also joined politics and become ministers. At least two became the Chief Ministers of the state. They were Rishang Keishing and W. Nipamacha Singh. Most of the M.Ps of Manipur started their career as teachers.

There are also several research institutes and centers run by the Central Government like ICAR, NEIST, IBSD, KVKs etc. It is not proposed to list the literary and scientific works produced by these institutions in this chapter.

Manipur has had always a powerful press. In the colonial period Hijam Irabot Singh was the first editor of a journal in Manipuri. Well known journals were *Lalit Manjuri Patrika, Yakairol* and *Bheigyabati Patrika*. Dr. N. Leiren Singh was the popular editor. Atombapu Sharma, the Sanskrit scholar was the editor of *Bheigyabati Patrika*. During the post-colonial period Keisam Kunjabihari Singh the brave editor of the *Ngasi Daily* should be remembered. Laisram Joychandra Singh founded the *Prajatantra*, an independent paper which survived more than half a century. Other party organs were *Simanta Patrika, Khollao, Anouba Samaj*, and *Sana Leibak*. There were English papers namely the *Manipur Mail* edited by a learned scholar and political leader who became a Member of Parliament of Manipur, Prof. N. Tombi Singh. The *Eastern Express* was edited by Laisram Jugeshwar Singh another Member of Parliament. Other English papers are *Imphal Free Press, The Sangai Express, Hueiyen Lanpao*. The later two had got Manipuri editions. *Hueiyen Lanpao* of the Manipuri edition was founded and edited by Salam Bharat Bhusan a remarkably fearless editor. Other newspapers are the popular *Poknapham, Iramdam, Toknga, Thoudang, Yakairol* etc.

There is an evening paper also. There are also tribal dialects papers like *Aza, Thujakna, Manipur Express* etc. Manipur had representatives of the news agency like PTI and UNI. Rajkumar Sanayaima was for many years a representative of PTI in Manipur. L. Joychandra, editor of the *Prajatantra* was the representative of UNI in Manipur. Several national newspapers like *Times of India*, the *Hindu, The Telegraph, The Pioneer, The Statesman* and *Assam Tribune* have their correspondents posted at Imphal. They are mostly local reporters well trained in journalism. There were several columnists on different aspects of knowledge on society and culture and even science who contributed regularly in local papers. Many university and college teachers wrote on the columns of these papers both English and Manipuri. Manipur journalists had a well organized union. They protected the interest of the papers and the reporters. The freedom of press in Manipur is due to these fearless journalists who always stand for freedom of expression.

The electronic media is quite alert in reporting the events of Manipur. The ISTV is the most popular electronic media in Manipur. In an insurgency ridden state like Manipur where both the security and the insurgents clash frequently the role of the media is extremely important. The media not only informs the people but influences the opinion of the people. The journalists constitute an important segment of the middle class in Manipur. They formed what is known as the fourth estate of the society. No society can exist without the press. The free press is a positive strength of the middle class in Manipur. The All India Radio and the Doordarshan Kendra have been rendering a yeoman's service to inform, educate and analyse the news for the people.

The Mercantile Class

During the colonial period the outside traders who settled down in Manipur monopolized both the internal and external trade constituted the mercantile class. There were frequent friction between the mercantile class and the indigenous people who were denied of trading facilities by the colonial authorities and the mercantile community. During the World War II the foreign mercantile community left the state and local people were compelled to do business and trade. The war also facilitated for the growth of contractors who carried out construction works for the army. After the war with the large scale funding through the payment of compensation, the local people started business and trade. The mercantile community returned after the war but they found that the local entrepreneurs had already come in to existence. After the merger and the introduction of the central rule the Indian officers favoured the outside mercantile communities in trade and business. At the same time they could not prevent the growth of local businessmen. Thus during the post colonial period a mercantile community consisting of Meitei businessmen and some tribal traders had emerged in Manipur. The emergence of the contractors led to emergence of an incipient class formation in Manipur. With the coming of statehood and political patronage made available to the local people many enterprising businessmen had become traders in consumer goods, contractors for construction works for the massive development projects in the state, starting of private transport system, participation in the managerial activities of the nationalized banks and cooperative banks which made capital available through both short term and long term loans brightened the prospect of growth of the businessmen, traders, shopkeepers, transport owners etc. They constituted the mercentill class.

Manipur is still an agrarian country. Despite the introduction of some scientific method of agriculture and improvement in the method of cultivation, Manipur's agriculture is not fully developed. While the valley has shown the improvement in agriculture the hill agriculture with its jhum system and terrace cultivation is still using the primitive method. The craftsmen who produce textiles and basketry and who indulge in carpentry and small machine shops do not have enough capital to become industrialists in any scale. Industrial development was very slow. The industries even in the small scale did not grow up. So it is left to the traders who influence the market economy of Manipur. They purchase goods from mainland India and sell it to the people of Manipur. Manipur has become a market for the manufacturing goods of mainland India. Private transport systems which carry goods and services to and from Manipur are to an extent successful. This mercantile community and the business community influence both the economy and politics of Manipur. There is now participation of contractor class in the democratic process of Manipur.

Artistes (Painting, Dance, Music and Drama)

Manipur is a land of dance, music and festivals. The people appreciate the artist who performs these arts. Traditionally Manipur was engaged in rituals and festivals. After conversion into Hinduism, singing of sankritana and Ras Leela became very popular. Lai Haraoba festivals provided venues for expression of the love for art. Therefore Manipur was abound in dancers, singers, drummers and performers of dance dramas. Therefore both during the colonial and post colonial period the artist constituted an important segment of the middle class. During the last days of 19th century and beginning of the 20th century, Manipur court encouraged the artists both painters and dancers. The famous painter N. Bhadra Singh who painted remarkable pictures of feudal and colonial Manipur was a well known name in Manipur. A large number of painters grew up in the post colonial period. The pioneer was Shyamo Sharma. The eminent painter was Rajkumar Chandrajit Singh who was well known by his brand R.K.C.S. Maharajkumar Priya Brata Singh was an impressionist painter. Haobam Shyamsunder Singh was both a painter and a sculptor. Thoidingjam Tombi Singh is a proficient abstract painter of the modern artistic school. The Imphal Art College is a well known art school in the state. The R.K.C.S. Art Gallery at Imphal is an important site for the lovers of painting to visit.

Every girl or woman is a dancer. They perform both the Ras Leela and the Lai Haraoba dance. The singers of the sanskritana during social and religious occasions were an important section of the society. Manipuri dance particularly the Ras Leela attracted the attention of Poet Rabindra Nath Tagore and he introduced Manipuri dance in his Santiniketan. Several gurus of Manipuri dances was employed in Viswa Bharati by Tagore. One of them was a young teacher named Maisnam Amubi Singh who became during the post colonial period a great exponent of Manipuri School of dances. It was Guru Maisnam Amubi Singh who contributed most to the perfection of Manipuri dance as one of the classical dances of India. There were other gurus of dance, music and songs. Rajkumar Priyogopalsana was an enthusiastic and passionate teacher of Manipuri dances both classical and folk. Many competent artists from Gauhati, Calcutta and Bombay learnt Manipuri dances from these competent gurus. Pandit Jawaharlal Nehru donated Rs.10,000/- for the establishment of a Dance College at Imphal. The present Manipur Jawaharlal Nehru Dance Academy run by Sangeet Natak Academy, New Delhi is the practical expression of Pandit Jawaharlal Nehru's vision. Thousands of students have been trained from this college. R.K. Singhajit of Triveni Kala Sangam of New Delhi was a living exponent of Manipuri School of dancing in the national capital. Dancing and singing are living tradition of Manipuri people.

Apart from dance and music which are performed during the religious rituals, drama is also developed in Manipur. Drama was introduced by the Bengali employees of Manipur state during the early colonial period. Maharaja Churachand Singh was a lover of dance, music and theatre. On his initiative, a scholar judge L. Iboongohal Singh wrote the first drama named Nar Singh in Manipuri and it was performed in the royal palace in 1926. Later on Hijam Irabot Singh established a theatre society known as Meitei Dramatic Union which was later renamed as the Manipur Dramatic Union. The MDU provided facilities for the performance of several dramas based on Manipur themes. Another theatre known as Aryan Theatre was established under the initiative of Arambam Dorendrajit Singh. After the Second World War theatre performances were very popular. The new theatre was the Rup Mahal. Therefore these three theatres, the MDU, the Aryan and the Rup Mahal became the leading theatre halls of Imphal. Theatres in small scales were performed in the villages of Manipur. During the National Drama Festival of 1954, the MDU Drama got the first prize. This national recognition gave lot of encouragement to the theatre personalities of Manipur playwright, actors and actresses. Choreography was a highly developed art. Theatre was used as a means of perpetuation of history, culture and tradition of Manipur. S. Lalit Singh was the famous director of MDU. M. Birmangol was a well known director of Aryan theatre. A. Shyamsunder, Hawaibam Nilamani, L. Netra were leaders of Rup Mahal Artist Union.

Manipur produced two distinguished drama personalities. One is Ratan Thiyam who was a former director of national School of Drama, a competent dramatist of international repute. Another was H. Kanhailal, a director and artist of great quality who had achieved applause from the drama world of India. Of the playwrights we can mention two names out of several writers. One was the legendry G.C. Tongbra who had written more than a hundred plays dealing with contemporary social and political problems of Manipur. He was awarded Padma Shri by the government of India and he was popularly known as the George Bernard Shaw of Manipur. Another playwright was Late Arambam Samarendra who wrote on the themes of contemporary problems of middle classes of Manipur. His *Judge Sahebki Imung* (The family of Judge Saheb) deals with pride and prejudice of a Meitei middle class. His *Chingnunggi Thawai* (Heart of the Hills) deals with the account of Jadonang and Rani Gaidinliu the legendary freedom fighter. The latter work won for him Dr. Ambedkar Award for Dalit literature. There are other playwrights in the state.

The artistes of the Sumang Leela group (Jatrawali) are an important part of the performing arts of Manipur. It is a part of popular folk theatre. If they are regarded as non manual workers the Sumang Leela artists fit into the middle class of the artists. There are many cultural organizations devoted to martial arts which had become a part of performing arts in Manipur. There grew up many organizations of singers and dancers. They provide livelihood to them. The talented artists who are film artist and film makers constitute a community of growing film industry. Manipur cinema has won both national and international awards. Shyam Sharma was most proficient film director of Manipur.

The Political Class

After the merger, Manipur was engaged in the struggle for restoration of democracy in the state. The period from 1949-1972 was a period of struggle for democracy which is known as the movement for statehood. Since Manipur got statehood in 1972, the next three decades was marked by working of the democracy in the administration of the state. During the first period Manipur passed through two stages of Chief Commissioner's Province or the Part C state and the Union Territorial Council. Manipur was provided an Advisory Council from 1952-1957. The members of the Advisory Council were appointed by the chief Commissioner from the political parties and independent distinguished persons. So under the Advisory Council, the members constituted the political class because they participated in the decision making of the administration. In 1952 there was election to the Parliament both House of Commons and Council of States (Rajya Sabha). There was election of 30 members to the electoral council. So the MPs and the members of the Electoral College influenced the political process in the state. From 1957 onwards Manipur was made a Union Territory with a 30 member council. There was election of the 30 members of the Council. All the members of the political parties both national and regional participated in the election. Three persons became Chairmen of the Territorial Council from 1957-1962. The members of the Territorial Council were equivalent to the members of the legislature. The members of the Territorial Council (known as TC members) were the legislators in a democracy which constituted the political class. Since 1972 Manipur had witnessed parliamentary elections which produced several M.Ps. Some of them became ministers in the central government. They were R.K. Jaichandra, Meijinlung Kamson and Th. Chaoba Singh. This political class included members of different political parties who were involved in the political agitations for statehood in Manipur. There were several tribal political parties in this political process.

In 1963, the Territorial Council was converted into a Territorial Assembly with a Council of ministers. The members of the Territorial Council were redesignated as Members of the Legislative Assembly (MLAs). There were ministers in the cabinet under one chief minister. Election to the Territorial Legislative Assembly was held in 1967 but the defection in the ministry led to the fall of the Congress party and introduction of President's Rule in November 1969. During the period there was All Party Political Agitation for statehood which was achieved in 1972. The TC members, the MLAs, the M.Ps, the ministers and the party leaders constituted the political class during the pre statehood days. However they did not command much respect and power because of the extreme powerful nature of the Chief Commissioner and Lt.Governor of the state.

During the post statehood days from 1972 to 2001 there were elections to the Legislative Assembly. Ministries were formed both by the regional parties and national parties. The most prominent of the regional parties was the Manipur People's Party followed by Manipur Hill Union and Manipur State Congress Party. The national political parties consisted of Indian National Congress, The Communist Party of India (CPI) and Bharatiya Janata Party (BJP). There were several Chief Ministers of the coalition ministries, cabinet ministers, minister of states, speakers and the members of the Assembly. There were a large number of party leaders, ideologue and workers of the national and regional parties. There were also members of the District Council in the hill areas, municipalities in urban areas and members of the Zilla Parishad and Gram Sabha of the Panchayats in the rural areas. These political bosses influenced the political decision regarding policies of administration. Therefore it is concluded that the chief ministers, ministers, MLAs, members of District Councils and Zilla Parishad constituted the political class which decided the political destiny of the state.

So the middle classes in Manipur by the end of the 20th century are fully developed. The classes which exist between the farmers who are the producers and the rulers who form the political class constitute the middle classes as described above.

NOTES

1. Quoted by William Easterly, *Journal of Economic Growth*, 2001, p. 317.
2. Quoted by Stuart M. Blumin, *The Emergence of Middle Class*; Social experience in the American city.
3. Andre Beteille, *The Indian Middle Class*, 2001.
4. B.B. Misra, *The Indian Middle Classes: Their Growth In Modern Times*, Oxford, 1961, p. 21.
5. Gurchain Singh, *The New Middle Class in India*, Jaipur, 1985, pp. 38 – 40.
6. *Ibid.*
7. B.B. Misra, *op cit,* p. 8
8. Ch. Manihar Singh, *A History of Manipuri Literature*, Sahitya Academy, 1996, p. 211 and see also R.K. Sanahal Singh (Ed) *Collected Works of Haodeijamba Chaitanya Singh in Manipuri*, Imphal, 1985.

9. Manipur State Archives, *Manipur State Durbar 1907-1047*, Imphal, 1987, pp. 3-5.
10. *Ibid.*
11. N. Lokendra Singh, *Unquiet Valley*, New Delhi, 1998, p. 113.

REFERENCES

1. Kshetri Bimola, *Politics and Government in Manipur*, Imphal, 2010.
2. N. Joykumar Singh, *From Colonialism to Democracy*, Guwahati, 2004.
3. B.B. Misra, *The Indian Middle Classes*, OUP, 1961.
4. N. Lokendra Singh, *The Unquiet Valley*, New Delhi, 1998.
5. K. Manimohan Singh, *Hijam Irabot Singh and his political movements*, New Delhi, 1986.
6. Ghanshyam Shah, 'Middle Class Politics: Case of anti reservation agitation in Gujarat', *Economic and Political Weekly*, Annual number, May, 1987
7. L.L. Aier, Contemporary Naga Social Formation and Ethnic Identity, New Delhi, 2006 deals with the evolution of Naga middle classes of Nagaland which have a similarity with the tribal middle classes of Manipur.
8. T.B. Bottomore, *Elites and Society*, London, 1964
9. T.B. Bottomore, *Classes in Modern Society*, London, 1965.
10. Stuart M. Blumin, *The Emergence of Middle Class: Social experience in American city, 1760-1900*, Cambridge University Press.
11. Concept note of the International Seminar on the Middle Class in India organized by the Indian Council of Social Science Research and Rajiv Gandhi Institute of Contemporary Studies, University of Mumbai, 12-14 June, 2009.

3

EMERGENCE OF THE TRIBAL MIDDLE CLASS IN MANIPUR: THE COLONIAL AND POST-COLONIAL PERIOD

Lal Dena

Historical Background

The hill areas of Manipur were peopled by two major ethnic groups—the Naga and the Kuki-Chin-Mizo, which are sub-divided into about thirty two smaller tribes according to difference in culture, language and customary practices. No clear-cut boundary line can be drawn between the areas occupied by the Nagas and the Kukis as they are all mixed up in all the hill districts except Churachandpur. In the present district of Ukhrul of north east Manipur, though the Tangkhul Nagas are predominant, a large number of Kukis also settle there. The Senapati district of north Manipur is inhabited by Chiru, Kom, Liangmei, Mao, Maram, Nepali, Paomei, Thangal and Zemei Naga while the two subdivisions of Kangpokpi and Saikul are predominantly inhabited by Kom, Koren and Thado Kuki. In the district of Tamenglong of west Manipur are found the following tribes— Chiru, Gangte, Kom, Hmar, Liangmei, Rongmei, Thado Kuki and Zemei Naga. The district of Chandel of south east Manipur is again inhabited by Aimol, Anal, Chothe, Lamkang, Monsang, Moyon, Thado and Zo and the Naga tribes appear to be in majority here. The district of Churachandpur of south Manipur is an exclusively Kuki-Chin-Mizo area.

Pre-colonial Social Structure

It is an established fact that the hill tribes, whether Naga or Kuki-Chins have come to their present habitat from different places of China or Southeast Asia through Burma and in different times. The earliest group came came probably between 11th and 13th century and the latest groups by the beginning of the 19th century. In course of their long migratory movement and sojourn at different places, the people had evolved a very stable and time-tested traditional institutions which can withstand the challenges of colonization and modernization. One prominent traditional institution which emerged in course of their onward migration was the chieftainship. Each village chiefdom was independent from one another. But one strking fact was the absence of any paramount tribal power, whether among the Kukis or the Nagas during the historical period.

It may be noted that every person could not become a chief. Only those persons who had the capacity to lead the people in their struggle for existence and constant anxiety in times of war, ability to command obedience from others, a certain charisma and readiness on the part of his followers to conform to the rules laid down by him, emerged as chiefs. Or such clan leaders who conquered new territories and built new villages were eventually recognized as chiefs. In each chiefdom, there was a village council. The specific character, composition and methods of functioning of the council deferred from tribe to tribe or from region to region. The chief was the supreme head of the council. The chiefs and the councilors in a sense constituted a privileged group in a traditional tribal society. The village council combined in itself both judicial and administrative powers. It settled disputes and cases, both civil and criminal according to customary laws.

There was no clear-cut class division in tribal society which may at most be characterized as a twofold category consisting of the commoners (cultivators) and the ruling chiefs. The two groups again represented two broad categories of livelihood: the commoners were the producers of food and the ruling chiefs appropriated a part of what the commoners had produced. As a matter of fact, the ruling chiefs practically depended on the labor of the common people. Particularly, the Chin-Kuki-Lushai people, in course of their historical evolution, had evolved an aged-old practice of *Busung-sadar* which may be considered as a sort of feudal tribute. According to this practice, every household cultivator within the chiefdom was to pay a certain fixed amount of paddy to the chiefs annually and every hind leg of any animal shot or killed in a trap was also surrendered to the chiefs. In between the chief and the commoners, there was no any other noticeable social group or class. This is to suggest that the concept of class in modern sense is very much conspicuous in its absence in pre-colonial tribal societies.

Emergence of Tribal Middle Class

Some scholars question the categorization of the newly emergent educated group as a middle class. They suggest that the newly emergent group may be identified as an 'elite class.' The term 'elite', according to them, suggests the superior status of its members. It also connotes positions of influence which the newly educated tribal leaders certainly held in redefining traditional values. Moreover, an 'elite' is an open group, access to which is not restricted by birth or family antecedents and modern education provides social mobility through which any one can rise up in the social ladder of tribal society. Another view contends that the newly western-educated group may be more appropriately called a 'middle class' because it occupied an intermediate position between the ruling colonial officials and the mass of the tribal population during the colonial period. Today the middle class is subdivided into lower middle class, centre middle class and upper middle class purely in terms of one's income. Both terms are used here interchangeably to mean the same class.

1. Impact of Colonial Administration

The emergence of tribal middle class was a colonial creation. The formal contact between the British colonial rule and the hill peoples can be said to begin at the beginning of the 19th century. In dealing with the hill peoples, the colonial officials adopted paternalistic attitude which was confined to the formal recognition of tribal chiefs who formed an integral part of colonial administration. In the wake of colonial administration, there came the opportunity of government services and small contract works and of course earning as labourer was already there. The subsistence barter economy was gradually replaced by monetized economy. To serve the needs of colonial establishment, recruitment of petty clerks, interpreters/translators, vaccinators, *lam subedars or lambus* were being made. Thus the colonial period saw the beginning of some people becoming rich and the introduction and extension of colonial administration in the hill areas of Manipur is the precursor for the emergence of tribal middle class in the hitherto classless tribal society.

2. *Introduction of Modern Education*

Closely connected with the colonial establishment was the Christian missionary who played a very important role in the establishment of schools which provided a material basis for the emergence of a new western-educated group. William Pettigrew, the first missionary, opened the first school in the hill areas at Ukhrul on 19 February, 1897 with 24 boys. Another 20 boys from a nearby village 4 miles south of Ukhrul joined the school later. Slowly few other boys from neighboring areas as far as Churachandpur and Tamenglong also joined the school. The first products of this Ukhrul School soon spread throughout the length and breadth of Manipur hills serving in different capacities as clerks in the sub-divisional headquarters of Churachandpur, Tamenglong and Ukhrul.

In the meantime, another Welsh missionary, Watkin R. Roberts, who was then working at the Welsh Mission medical clinic at Aizawl came to Senvon and his undenominational mission soon covered the whole of Southern Manipur. Education being the most powerful instrument of Christian proselytism, almost everywhere there had been mushroom growth of schools and the once ignorant tribal masses also had began to eat the fruit of the tree of knowledge of good and evil.

On the northern side, the American Baptist Mission had shifted its mission station to Kangpokpi with a leprosy hospital there. In this way, the missionary movement had assumed a new dimension covering elementary medical education and other philanthropic works also. But conspicuous was the deliberate negligence of secondary education for which a tribal student had to go to the valley or other neighboring states for further studies. Opportunity for education and earning money was open for all in the hills. Whoever could afford to get elementary education was believed to know even the number of a tree-leave by putting his foot at its ground. Thus out of this newly educated group emerged teachers, evangelists, new church leaders (pastors) and political leaders.

3. *Tribal Middle Class: Its Orientation and Ideology*

Having explained the historical roots of tribal middle class, let us now look into their behavior and ideology. The colonizers and the Christian missionaries taught the newly emergent leaders that they were 'backward' and should accept the colonial rule as beneficial. This is the argument which was carefully used for justifying colonial occupation. The missionaries thus taught the people that they were 'savages' and should accept new concepts of Christian ethics and western values without even examining whether there was anything of permanent value in the culture and traditions of the tribal society.

One of the main objectives of the missionaries was to train native workers and operate through them. Every new convert was under obligation to abandon his old faith and habits and to give up his tribal hair-cut and to adopt the European hair style. What was most crucial here was the change in their mental outlook. The western-educated group looked at Europeans as models and tended to become pro-western in outlook and attitude. They also began to look with disgust at their own culture through the glasses of their new masters who framed the syllabus and content of the teaching they received. The profound but devastating psychological effect the colonial rule and mission education had on young men educated in their schools cannot be ignored. These young men felt and preached that their ancestors were 'headhunters', and made other young men ashamed of their past, their way of living, their tradition and culture. They also felt that the 'western' people and their so-called 'civilizing mission' had brought them into the 'light'. This is not to ignore the fact that the impact of western civilization upon the people was only skin-deep and mere acceptance of superficial western values does not make one 'civilized'.

One contradictory situation in which the new educated group was caught was that they were still bound by some traditional values and customs. Their main problem was, therefore, the simultaneous adaptation of two mentally contradicting elements: one 'traditional' and the other 'western'. In the process, they were neither western nor traditional but an incorporation of both.

What is significant here is that the Christian missionaries educated the people and trained native workers who began to regard themselves as belonging to a more or less different category and assumed new leadership as educators, administrators, spiritual leaders, political leaders, etc., thereby disturbing the traditional social organizational structure and also affecting the economic interests of the traditional leaders. In fact, at the initial stage, there arose a conflict between the two leaderships: the traditional leaders upholding the existing institutions and practices and the new leaders tending to condemn traditional values though they were still bound by the very same traditional values and customs. Both of them, however, played more or less the same roles. The new leaders acted as a bridge between the colonial administration and indigenous population by serving, apart from their normal duties as teachers and preachers, as translators or interpreters particularly during the First and the Second World Wars.

As new political consciousness dawned upon the people at the beginning of the 20th century, new political leaders began to question even the very basis of colonial domination. With the acceptance of democracy as a form of government and consequently, adult franchise, they began to negate colonial administration and question the rights and privileges of the traditional leaders who were dubbed as 'lackeys of the colonial government'. This is not to say that they were opposed to perceived ideals and principles of western institutions. In fact, it was through the acceptance of these ideals that they claimed their right to leadership. As a result they lacked firm legitimacy in the society in which they lived. Whatever legitimacy they claimed, tended to become 'alien' (without firm traditional roots). They, like the church leaders, denounced tradition as a basis for legitimacy. They were against the colonial personnel and traditional leaders but not western ideals and principles. In their fight against the colonial rulers and their close collaborators (the traditional rulers), the political leaders appealed to the sentiments of the people by forming various ethnic based political parties. Such parties exerted a strong appeal and there was inevitably a popular reaction against traditional leaders. The political leaders demanded democratization of traditional political institutions, which meant the abolition of chieftainship and village councils with their feudal-like servitudes such as the *busung-sadar* and forced labor. The Mizo Union movement (1946-1948) in Manipur and Mizoram was a case in point.

4. Modern Tribal Middle Class in Post-colonial India

Though the progress of education was slow in the hill areas of Manipur, a second generation of tribal elite had emerged in tribal society in the 50s after India's independence in 1947. Growth of modern education and monetary economy went together hand in hand. The Government of India also introduced the scheduled system through which those section of people who are born in a caste-ridden Hindu society are classified as 'scheduled castes' and those tribes outside the caste system are included in the category of 'scheduled tribes' with a fixed quota of reserved posts for entry into the civil services, legislative assemblies and parliament. Out of these second generation tribal elite, different types of new leadership had emerged. New political leadership cutting across existing state boundaries had demanded right of self-determination and in some extreme cases even secession from India. New professional group who entered into government services through reserved quota began to constitute the top class and cream of the tribal population. At the same time, a host of theology-oriented church leaders and the nouveau riche from among the business communities and contractors formed themselves into a powerful group which cannot be easily reckoned with.

The third generation children of these tribal leaders could now afford to get better opportunities to study even outside the state of Manipur. So in course of time these educated people are firmly placed in government jobs and as a matter of fact, many of them began to enter into All-India services such as civil service, police service, medical service, engineering service, forest service, etc. Again the fourth generation children of these central services holders or nouveau riche, being born and brought up in metropolitan cities, begin to join the best colleges and universities in the country and can even compete with non-tribal candidates in the all-India competitive examinations. Elite marriage is also confined to the families of similar status and thereby building the solid base for a permanent middle class in tribal society. The competition is also no longer between the children of this class and the children of the interior villages in the hills; but is now among the children of the same middle class families themselves. Therefore while the reservation system is acting as a means for bringing up the weaker section to the level of other advanced section of the society, it is at the same time creating a new privileged group within the tribal society

5. *Modern Tribal Middle Class vis-à-vis Tribalism or Detribalization*

Surprisingly the tribal middle class in the post-colonial period are caught in two self-contradictory situations. While they are in the process of detribalization, they are at the same time advocates of tribalism. As a matter of fact, tribalism emerges in a situation where tribes and tribesmen are vanishing. This is to say that tribalism flourishes among the detribalized middle class which includes politicians, bureaucrats, teachers, doctors, church leaders, wealthy businessmen and contractors. In order to distinguish themselves from the rest of the indigenous masses, they tend to uncritically imitate modern values and life-styles. More crucial, all of the members of the elite have left their ancestral land to settle in town or cities. In this way, disparity between the elite and rural masses has also become wider than before. They also tend to look with disgust at their established traditional values and customs. What is important is the change in their mental outlook. They think and act as other non-tribal urbanized people do, beginning to impose upon themselves heavy bourgeois values.

In a sense, every professional tribal is detribalized as soon as he leaves his tribal area. He begins to live in different kinds of social groupings, earns his livelihood in a different way and comes under different authorities. But the question is: is he really free from the influences of his tribe? In this connection, Gluckman argues that urbanization does not necessarily disrupt tribal solidarity. It is true that a tribal who lands up in a town or city, becomes isolated from his ethnic environment. But it always happens that even there he continues to live with his fellow tribesmen and this can strengthen his communal or tribal ties(Markovizt: 1970). For instance, different tribal groups settle permanently in different parts of Imphal, Guwahati, Bangaluru, Calcutta, Delhi, Mumbai, etc. Even in those metropolitan cities, they continue to organize themselves on the basis of tribes or communities. Because the spirit of tribe always exists as traditional law on cultural rituals and rites regarding death, intergenerational social relationship, leadership and the positions of elders and youth in society. Ethnic-based political parties or voluntary associations are always the visible operational arms of tribalism. These are again instruments for the development of ethnic nationality. Very often, the leadership of these ethnic-based parties or associations is drawn from the detribalized elite who at the same time form a part of national elite in a wider context. They identify themselves with the state and its government. Yet, as and when occasion demands, the detribalized elitists use these parties or associations to protect or promote their own communal interests. For this reason, they are unable to separate themselves from the wishes of their kin and the demands of belonging to their tribe. In a way, "tribe affects the individual at a very personal level. Tribe is touchable. Tribe is not mysterious. Tribe has a face. Tribe is nurturing. Tribe has tradition and culture. Tribe is the clear answer for many people to the question 'who am I?"(B.S. Aswal, 2012:95).

To a great extend, tribalism is the outcome of conflicts between segments of detribalized elites in a pluralistic society. Because of the very nature of inner contradictions inherent in the class relationship, one ethnic group always tries to dominate or compete with the other tribal group. A ministry or government in which one ethnic group is dominant, is often suspected to favor that ethnic group at the expense of others. In this way, we see both competition and conflict for power and position among rival ethnic groups.

According to Peter P. Ekeh, University of Ibadan, Nigeria, tribalism is the direct result of the dialectical confrontation between the two publics: primordial public and civic public. The primordial public is closely identified with primordial groupings, sentiments and activities. Whereas the civic public is based on civil structure: the military, the civil service, the police, etc. The leaders of the primordial public should not be confused with ethnic leadership. They want to channelize a great share of resources from the civic public to individuals or to his community as they can.

The protagonists of tribalism strengthen the positive value of ethnic loyalty. They also create in many cases, cohesive groups much larger than those that existed in the pre-colonial era. For instance, the concept of Nagaisation is still an expanding and unending process and some tribes who are more akin to the Kuki-Mizo groups linguistically and culturally, are now in the process of being Nagaised. Among the Kuki-Mizo groups also, the search for a more accommodating nomenclature is still on and options opened for them are: Kukiaisation, Zomiasation or Mizoaisation. The Paites, the Vaipheis, the Zous, and Simtes, etc. tend to opt for Zomi. Whereas the Hmars in and outside Mizoram prefer to identify themselves as Mizo by still retaining their identity as Hmar. The Gangtes, as a matter of fact, have recently merged with the Mizos.

In the final analysis, tribalism, good or bad, ensures ethnic loyalty which in its turn, provides for the tribal people a sense of their identity and the values of their culture and tradition. At the same time it also provides a material basis for political and socio-religious separatist movements. Even church organizations are based on tribal lines. The whole tragedy with most of the tribal Christians is that their ethnic loyalty often transcends their commitment to Christianity. The majority of them are tribals first and Christians second. In this way, the process of tribalism and detribalization are dove-tailing in a changing tribal society today.

Tribalism or Detribalization?

Tribalism has become one of the major ills of the state. It is mostly used in its derogatory sense, as a term of abuse - like 'bourgeois', 'capitalist' or 'communist' (in their derogatory senses) are used in other parts of the world. In any state with multi-ethnic groups or tribes, inter-tribal relationships have always played an important role in social development. Such inter-tribal relationships can assume different characteristics and have sometimes been reduced to tribalism. There is now a tendency even among social scientists to attribute to tribalism everything reactionary that is affecting national unity.

1. Conceptual Problem

What, after all, is tribalism? The term is vague and its current usage embodies a number of different concepts. One may describe a person as a 'tribalist' if he adheres to the norms of his traditional society, however inappropriate those norms may be, to the modern situation. Others use the term to describe a person who adapts his behavior to modern situations, yet retains his ethnic loyalty which parallels or transcends loyalty to the state. For instance, a person belonging to a Hmar tribe in Manipur owes his allegiance or loyalty to both of community and the state of Manipur. But at the same time he is also a member of a wider ethnic-based organization like the Hmar Inpui (Hmar Supreme House) which cuts across state boundaries and in such a case, his loyalty to his community may sometimes transcend his loyalty to the state of his birth.

In another sense, tribalism may also mean a hostile attitude to members of some other ethnic group. It is a kind of folk expression signifying fear that one group is establishing, or trying to establish, dominance over others. It may also mean a policy directed to granting certain favors and privileges to persons who belong to the same ethnic group of a leader, and to subsidizing development plans for one's own area and so on.

Writing in the African context, Abner Cohen, a noted sociologist, argues that tribalism is the result, not of ethnic groups disengaging themselves from one another after independence, but of increasing interaction between them within the context of the new political situation. It is the outcome, not of conservation, but of dynamic socio-cultural changes brought about by the new cleavages and new alignments of power within the framework of a new state. Tribalism is thus to a large extent an urban modern phenomenon, and one which develops with increasing modernization of the tribal economy. According to others, tribalism is a political expression of a form of consciousness characteristic of the stage of class formation. Still some other scholars understand it very broadly, "as an aggregate of surviving archaic institutions and organizations associated with the tribal system, like kinship, forms of inheritance, traditional ceremonies and customs, the strength of bonds of blood relationship, a sense of ethnic solidarity and so on". From the given diversified views, it is quite clear that tribalism which is a complex urban phenomenon, has the following characteristics: (a) primordial attachment to the basic tribal systems - kingship, inheritance, traditional ceremonies and customs which are strong bonds of blood relationship; (b) ethnic loyalty or ethnic solidarity; (c) tribal elitist conflict and competition among different ethnic groups within the framework of emerging socio-economic situations.

2. *Tribalism or Detribalization*

Surprisingly enough, tribalism emerges in a situation where tribes and tribesmen are vanishing. This is to say that tribalism flourishes among the detribalized elites, which include politicians, bureaucrats, university and college teachers, doctors, church leaders, wealthy businessmen and contractors. In order to distinguish themselves from the rest of the indigenous masses, the elite group tends to uncritically imitate western or modern values and life-styles. It also tends to look with disgust at their established traditional values and life-styles. What is important is the change in their mental outlook. They think and act as other urbanized people do, beginning to impose upon themselves heavy bourgeois values. They are thus placed in a contradictory situation - the simultaneous adaptation to two mentally contradicting elements: one traditional and the other 'western'.

3. *Consequences of Tribalism*

In a sense, every professional tribal is detribalized as soon as he leaves his tribal area. He begins to live in different kinds of social groupings, earns his livelihood in a different way and come under different authorities. But the question is: is he really free from the influences of his tribe? In this connection, Bluckman argues that urbanization does not necessarily disrupt tribal solidarity. It is true that a person who lands up in a town or city, becomes isolated from his ethnic environment. But it always happens that even there he continues to live with his fellow tribesmen and this can strengthen his communal or tribal ties.

For instance, different tribal groups settle permanently in different parts of Imphal, Calcutta, Delhi, etc. They continue to organize themselves on the basis of tribes or communities. Ethnic-based political parties or voluntary associations are always the visible operational arms of tribalism. These are again instruments for the development of ethnic nationality. Very often, the leadership of these ethnic-based parties or associations is drawn from the detribalized elites who at the same time form a part of national elite in a wider context. They identify themselves with the state and its government. Yet, as and when occasion demands, the detribalized elitists use these parties or associations to protect or promote their own communal interests.

This is to say that tribalism is the outcome of conflicts between segments of detribalized elites in a pluralistic society. Because of the very nature of inner contradictions inherent in the class relationship, one ethnic group always tries to dominate or compete with the other tribal group. A cabinet or government, in which one ethnic group is dominant, is suspected to favor that ethnic group at the expense of others. In this way, we see both competition and conflict for power and position among rival ethnic groups.

According to Professor Peter P. Ekeh, University of Ibadan, Nigeria, tribalism is the direct result of the dialectical confrontation between the two publics: primordial public and civic public. The primordial public is closely identified with primordial groupings, sentiments and activities. Whereas the civic public is based on civil structure: the military, the civil service, the police, etc. The leaders of the primordial public should not be confused with ethnic leadership. They want to channelize as great a share of resources from the civic public to individuals or to his community as they can.

The protagonists of tribalism strengthen the positive value of ethnic loyalty. They also create in many cases, cohesive groups much larger than those that existed in the pre-colonial era. For instance, the concept of Nagaisation is still an expanding and unending process and some tribes who are more akin to the Kuki-Mizo groups linguistically and culturally, are now in the process of being Nagaised. Among the Kuki-Mizo groups also, the search for a more accommodating nomenclature is still on and the options opened for them are: Kukiaisation, Zomiasation and Mizoaisation. The Paites, the Vaipheis, the Zous, and Simtes, etc. tend to opt for Zomi. Whereas the Hmars in and outside Mizoram prefer to identify themselves as Mizo by still retaining their identity as Hmar. The Gangtes, as a matter of fact, have recently merged with the Mizos.

In the final analysis, tribalism, good or bad, ensures ethnic loyalty which in its turn, provides for the tribal people a sense of their identity and the values of their culture and tradition. At the same time it also provides a material basis for political and socio-religious separatist movements. Even church organizations are based on tribal lines. The whole tragedy with most of the tribal Christians is that their ethnic loyalty often transcends their commitment to Christianity. The majority of them are tribals first and Christians second. In this way, the process of tribalism and detribalization are dove-tailing in the changing tribal society today.

The patterns of leadership in Hmar society of Manipur and be analyzed in its historical perspective and discussed in the context of the different stages and periods of evolution of that society beginning with the food gathering stage and passing through (a) the stage when they evolved a certain primitive technology of production and began settling down in Manipur, (b) the stage when the people came under colonial rule by 1891, and (c) the post colonial stage. The leadership may be classified into three of its different manifestations: traditional, religious and political.

1. Traditional Leaders

Traditional leaders include the chief (lal), the councilors (muolkilmitha/ khawnbawl-upa), the priests (thiempu) and the youth commanders (val-upa). Their social foundation was based on customs and tradition and are, in fact, guardians/keepers/ spokesmen/interpreters of customary and traditional laws. The sphere in which they operate is limited to what may be called chiefdom or village-based society. This kind of leadership still functions at some level side by side with the religious and political leaders, though the latter are more predominant in the day-to-day affairs of Hmar society. There are complexities of social, economic, political and historical situations in which such leaders emerged and operated. The emergence of a leader, his action or behavior and his position in a society, whether 'primitive' or 'civilized' must have been conditioned by the manner in which that society met and satisfied its material needs and engaged itself in productive activity.

The autocratic position of the chief can further be demonstrated by the manner in which the councilors, priests and youth commanders were selected or appointed. The councilors were normally selected or appointed by the chief from a wealthy and influential group of persons who were also senior members of various sub-clans. Thus, the chief and the councilors in a sense constituted a privileged group in a traditional Hmar society, and the village council through which they operated tended to serve their narrow and vested interests. An interesting feature of this development is that these positions became hereditary.

2. *Traditional Priests*

Within the hierarchical power structure, the priest occupied a vital position. The source of his authority lay on the assumption that he could control certain natural phenomena: epidemics, floods, droughts, famines, etc., all of which loomed large and affected their means of livelihood and production. Ignorance and inability to comprehend the objective laws of nature made the people easy victims of exploitation at the hands of the priest. The priest had dual functions: religious and secular. As far as religious functions were concerned, the priest was supreme and particularly in the case of epidemics, he could even influence the chief and his councilors. He acted as a mediator between the people and god (pathien). He offered prayers for the prosperity of crops, performed sacrifices for the sick and the dead and also sanctified the village from the influence of demons and evil spirits. In so far as his secular function was concerned, he would be called upon to decide those cases which the village council could not decide due to want of evidence. The priest, particularly the chief's priest (lal thiempu), was nominated by the chief and he practically depended upon the labour which people would render to him for his services. The traditional leaders thus devised means by which they kept themselves in power and perpetuated this state of affairs in their own interest.

3. *Youth Leadership (Valupa)*

Another group of leaders who exerted considerable influence upon society were the youth commanders (val-upa) who operated through the institution of buonzawl (bachelors' dormitory). The buonzawl served as a sort of military wing of the village organization by imparting strict discipline and vigorous training in the art of tribal warfare and defence to youngsters (except women) above fifteen years old. In times of peace, the youth commanders mobilized the youth and rendered free and compulsory services to the society. The youth commanders were normally people who had made outstanding contributions to the society. Their activities were regulated in such a manner as to serve the interest of the chief and the village. This is, however, not to ignore the fact that the chiefs and the councilors could at times be subject to the will of the youth.

Surprisingly enough, the role and even the basis of the relationship between the youth commanders and the youth has remained intact despite the tremendous impact of Christianity and modern education provided by the missionaries. Even though the buonzawl fell victim to western influence, the youth commanders still play a crucial role in Hmar society and the modern survival of youth commanders can be attributed to the fact that they are indispensable for such social occasions as death, marriage, etc., and it is they who can effectively mobilize the youth for community services.

Political Leadership

With the introduction of the Manipur Hill Village Authority Act of 1956, the traditional authorities were legally dethroned but their influence was not completely eliminated. Since the institution of chieftainship had taken deep roots in society, the traditional authorities, particularly the chiefs, are still accepted as legitimate in the eyes of the people and in fact continue to function as ex-officio chairmen in the village authority councils, interpreting and administering traditional laws and customs. Hence, complete abolition of chieftainship is not possible because of its value as a symbol of established authority and its ritual function as judge in matters such as local disputes over land, marriage, divorce, cattle, inheritance, rights regarding property, etc. So there is no doubt that the traditional leaders still have considerable influence over the masses because of the fact that they have closer contact with them. The political leaders cannot therefore ignore them. Since the church leaders also have a well-knit organization and have a hold on the people in religious matters, the political leaders cannot ignore them either. At the time of elections, the political leaders seek the co-operation of the church leaders and the traditional leaders. Though the political leaders profess to work for the establishment of a secular democracy, their reliance on church leaders and the traditional leaders in a sense perpetuates the survival of these types of leadership.

The leadership structure in Hmar society is thus based on a three tier system: traditional, religious and political. The modern political leaders cut across clan organizations of Hmar society. There seems to be two contradictory forces at work here; the modern political leader is normally perceived to be above clan considerations and looked upon as a leader of the tribe vis-à-vis other tribes and communities whereas clan-consciousness remains an important consideration in intra-personal relationships within the Hmar society. The basic social organizational unit is still the clan and clan-consciousness seems to be growing stronger than before. The emergence of a political leadership and also the church leadership is due to the colonial experience and the education provided by Christian missions, coupled with the forces working within the premises of traditional Hmar society. Consciousness of moral imperatives aimed at economic and social reconstruction seems therefore to be more or less absent within the leadership. This is so, particularly in the case of political leadership. The moral imperatives which characterized the relationship between the leader and the people in the early stages have gradually begun to disappear. If, however, there is a primordial social obligation, it is only a façade and is intended to get maximum personal benefit by getting political and administrative control. Having obtained this control, the political leaders tend to narrow down the community's interest to personal self-interest and more seriously, they begin to live in urbanized towns thereby gradually losing whatever contact they have with the masses. The result is that the ordinary individual of the backward Hmar society has fallen victim to the machinations of the different types of leaderships.

REFERENCES

1. B.S. Aswal, *Tribal and Human Rights*, Cyber Tech Publications, New Delhi, 2012.
2. Gluckman, 'Tribalism in Modern British Central Africa' in I.L. *Markovitz's African Politics and Society*, Free Press, New York, 1970.
3. Lal Dena, 'Detribalized Elite Groups: Their behaviour' in Souvenir, NEIHA Third Annual Session, Imphal, 1982.
4. P.C.Lloyd, *Africa in Social Change*, Penguin Books, 1972.
5. Peter E.Ekeh, 'Colonialism and the two publics in Africa: A Theoretical Statement' in *Comparative Studies in Society and History*, Vol. 17, Camdridge.
6. R.M.Ismagilova, *Ethnic Problems of the Tropical Africa. Can they be Solved?*
7. G.A.Grierson, *Linguistic Survey of India*, Vol.III, Part III, Kolkata, 1904.
8. Alexander Mackenzie, *History of the Relations of the Government with the Hill Tribes of the North East Frontier of Bengal*, Kolkata, 1884.
9. Philip Mason, Patterns of Dominance, Oxford University Press, London, 1970.
10. Rochunga Pudaite, *The Education of the Hmar People*, Sielmat, Churachandpur, 1963.
11. Nari Rastomji, *Enchanted Frontiers*, Oxford University Press, London, 1973.
12. John Shakespeare, *The Lushai-Kuki Clans*, Macmillan, 1912.
13. Hranglien Songate, *Hmar Chanchin (Hmar History)*, Churachandpur, Reprint, 1977.
14. C.A.Soppit, *A Short Account of the Lushai-Kuki Tribes of North Eastern Frontier with an Outline Grammar*, Shillong, 1887.

4

THE EMERGENCE OF THE MIDDLE CLASSES IN THE POLITICS OF MANIPUR

N. Joykumar Singh

The concept of class is the outcome of the division in the society which is created by the inequalities among the people of the given social life. Such type of phenomenon is created either by natural or economic. But if the nature of the social division is to be observed very carefully it can be suggested that the influence of economic inequality has played a great role in the process of the making of social division. In this respect it can be said that the differences of relationship which a person or group bears to property or means of production and distribution also has played a big role in the process of the creation of inequalities among the members of the given society. It is a known fact that if an individual is a landowner he tends to exercise a relatively superior social significance and on the other hand if he is a mere tiller of the soil that does not belong to him, he finds himself socially scaled down. This is the general principle which applies to all the areas of the economic production. The general principle which determines the quality of social honour is based on the total economic factor which is earned by a person as his income. Because it relates to the physical size of the means capable of acquiring interest in property. A difference of income produces hierarchy of prestige and power according to the variation of its size. At the same time it also produces qualitative change in the status of an individual or group only when it is converted into a form affecting relationship to property.

Indeed, the status of the class concept is not a new phenomenon. Karl Marx was the first man who made a successful attempt to explain or define the concept of class from the materialistic point of view in a more expressive way. It is said that "classes are large group of people differing for each other by the place they occupy in the historically determined system of social production, by their relation (in most cases fixed and formulated in laws) to the means of production by their role in the social organisation of labour, and consequently, by the dimension of the share of which they dispose and mode of acquiring it"[1] From this observation it is also suggested that the existence of 'Class' is associated with historically determined mode of production. Lenin also said that classes are a group of people one of which can appropriate the labour of another owing to the different places they occupy in a definite system of social economy[2]. It is also mentioned that the development of the social division by labour and the appearance of private ownership of the means of production are the only determining factor for the emergence of class. It is suggested that it may not be very much difficult to give class analysis of the capitalist society.

But surprisingly in all his historical writings Marx did not give a precise definition of the term 'middle class'. In his book 'The class struggle' in France 1848-1850 Marx had categorized the classes in society into six groups. They are (i) Financial bourgaoisie (ii) Industrial bourgeoisie (iii) Petty bourgeoisie (iv) Peasants (v) Proletariate and (vi) Leamper proletariate. Again in his book on 'Revolution and Counter Revolution in Germany' he again divided the society into seven groups. They are (i) feudal, (ii) nobility (iii) bourgeoisie (iv) petty bourgeoisie (v) rich and middle peasants (vi) agricultural labour and (vii) industrial works. But no mention was made of the 'middle class' as such. In this context it can also be suggested that apart from the economic inequalities the civil and political inequalities of man had also produced a division in the whole body of the society. It consists of the different privileges which some men enjoy to the exclusion of the other. It is a known fact that in a society some are rich, honoured and powerful, while other are not though there are no differences in natural qualities. Thus society is divided into classes or group of people by joining together from the motive of common economic interest, common ways of behaviour and common traits of character. Each such class forms as heirarchy of status according to the varying quality of social prestige and power expressed through the standard of living, nature of occupation and wealth.

Whatever the case may be the term 'middle class' is a new concept in the class division of the society which was developed mainly due to the growth of complexity in the production relations. It is a well known fact that at a particular stage of social life the social stratification was based either on caste which were hereditary or privilege group in their respective society. But in course of time the social stratification particularly in modern times implies economic classes created as a result of the prevalent mode of production and resultant property relation. There is a high degree of occupational mobility which in turn leads to social mobility. Therefore the modern social classes are not like the mutually exclusive status group of the past. Rather one can raise in the social ladder depending on one's success in economic life. From this angle it is observed that the middle class is heterogeneous social order which contains different functional and occupational groups. The growth of the system of the salary receipt which is popularly known as 'white collar job' represents a new class i.e, middle class in the society. It comprises office workers, supervisors technicians and innumerable others. V.M. Dandekar in his work on 'Nature of class conflict in Indian society' said that these new groups are essentially a product of capitalist development[3] Indeed, from the context of India's social division it is a product of colonial legacy. From this context Dandekar even said that perhaps Max himself did not anticipate the emergence and growth of this class.

But it is a claimed that Marx had already pointed out the existence of middle class. According to Marx middle class is a group of section of the society who stands between the workers on the one hand and the capitalists and landlord on the other."[4] It is also said that "economically, socially, politically or ideologically middle classes do not represent single whole"[5] because they occupy a unique place in the class structure of a society anywhere between the bourgeoisie and proletariat. Like the capitalists they own private property and like workers they live largely through their own labour rather than exploitation. In a sense they are the working people, wage earners just like industrial workers. The people who belong to this group live on their income without producing social value. It is further argued that the middle class people do not contribute so much to the social stability.

Whatever the case may be the emergence of middle class group in the social life is a significant development. In the present context they play a major role in the whole political and economic life of any given society. B.B. Misra in his work makes a successful attempt to analyze the middle class into five categories. They are (i) the commercial middle class (ii) the industrial middle class (iii) the educated middle class (main objective of western education) (iv) the landed middle class and (v) the educated middle class (learned profession).[6]

The introduction of western system of education may be marked as the beginning of the emergence of middle class in the system of social division. Right for the early period of time the people of Manipur had enjoyed the practice of the feudal society. Under the framework of feudalism the people in the society was confined broadly into two groups. One was the privileged group who belonged to the core area of the feudal lords and another was the peasants. But the establishment of relationship with the British and their gradual influence in the day to day administration of the state had produced a far reaching impact in the ongoing social life of the people of Manipur. Like any other countries Manipur had little activities in the field of commercial and industrial areas. No doubt she had the experience of small scale marketing relationship with the people of surrounding hill areas that too particularly within her own territory. The same condition also existed in the case of industry. Therefore since she had little activities in these areas there were no significant impact in the social life of the people. But the introduction of western or modern system of education had produced a large scale impact in the stratification of the social life of the people of Manipur. The growth of formal education system had rendered a great contribution towards the growth of 'educated middle class' in the state. These groups of people played a great role in the changing political, social and economic scenario of the state in the course of the future history of this place.

Since the educated people formed the basic platform of the growth of middle class in Manipur their role in the changing phenomena is a very important part in the history of the state. Therefore the main objective of this paper is to make a humble attempt to analyze the nature of their growth as middle section of the society and their contribution in the changing scenario of the state of Manipur. One of the basic objective of the introduction of western education system in India by the British colonial authority, as observed by the nationalist writers, was to train the Indian people in order to suit in the colonial administrative system. But according to the colonial writers the basic objective of the introduction of western education was to make the Indian officers of Government intellectually and morally fit to perform their duties with efficiency. No doubt the introduction of western system of education particularly in the context of India had produced a good impact for the emergence of the educated middle class. B.B. Misra said, educated middle class meant a new group of persons who received higher education through the medium of English and engaged in the various recognized professions that grew in modern times as a result of western education and capitalist economy[7]. The foundation for the growth of educated middle class was laid down in Manipur from the last quarter of the 19th century at the initiative of the British officials. Before the emergence of the influence of the British there were no formal education system in Manipur. Due to this reason education, in the real sense of the term, was not very popular and it was confined only to the selected few people in the society. No doubt Manipur have her own script and accordingly writing and reading system already existed right from the early period of time. But, as mentioned above that due to the lack of the system of large scale education system the people took less interest in this field. However there is evidence about the existence of the so called 'Gurukul' system of education. Under this system only the interested persons went to the houses of the teachers for getting writing, and reading knowledge etc.

But just after the emergence of the influence of the modern system of education, that too at the initiative of the British, the people had started to give importance in this area. The formal establishment of relationship between Manipur and British East India Company was done in the year 1762. But the influence of the British was not able to penetrate until the outbreak of 'Seven years Devastation (Chahi Taret Khuntakpa) in 1819. A strong influence of the British was started to enter in every aspects of the life of the society of Manipur just after the liberation from the hands of Burma in the year 1826. The First Anglo-Burmese War came to an end with the Treaty of Yandaboo in the year 1826. And the official relationship between Manipur and British War started from the year 1835 with the opening of the office of the British Political Agent in Manipur. Due to the instability in the political life of the country the King of Manipur also had started to take help from the office of the Political Agent. Taking the advantage of this situation the British also started to pay attention in every aspect of the administration of the state.

Still it is exactly not known about the year of the establishment of the first education system on the line of the western education. It is mentioned that in the year 1872 the Bengal government sent stationary items including books of worth Rs. 400/500 to Manipur with an objective to start school and accordingly a new school was established in the state[8]. Except this information nothing was mentioned about the location of the school and number of students enrolled in this new school and the name of the teacher and also about the response of the common people. It is also said that the British had brought the Bengali script and language along with the introduction of western education system in Manipur. The policy of the British was not acceptable to the people. Because they felt that the introduction of Bengali script and language perhaps, might have led to the extinction of traditional script of the state[9]. Then in the year 1885 Sir James Johnstone, the then British Political Agent in Manipur, established a middle English school. The establishment of this school may be treated as the basic foundation for the growth of educated middle class people in Manipur. As a first step the school building was constructed inside the campus of the office of the Political Agent. (Present campus of the Governer of the State). As it has already mentioned above about the hesitative nature of the people when the British tried to introduce Bengali script and language in the newly establish school. Therefore most of the people paid less response to the efforts of the British for the growth of the modern education system. This alarming situation was continued till the outbreak of Anglo-Manipur War of 1891.

The war came to an end with a victory in favour of the British. Immediately after getting victory the British had established direct colonial administration. Along with this new administrative arrangement the British officials in Manipur again made an effort to regenerate the movement for the introduction of modern education system which was started from the year 1885. The Middle English school which was established by James Johnston was again rebuilt at the central Khwairamban market and it was officially opened on 1st June 1892[10] and thus on the 31st March 1893 the strength of the number of the students reached to 113 (one hundred thirteen). In the same year another school of lower primary level was established at Sekmai village. Thus the activities of the movement for the growth of English education system was tremendously increased. In the year 1885 there were one school in Manipur. But in the year 1895 the number of schools increased to six. They were three in Imphal, two in the Valley and one in the Hill area. At the same time the number of students also increased in an encouraging degree.

In the year 1910 Manipur had produced her first student who passed matric examination under the Calcutta University. His name was Wahengbam Yumjao Singh. This was a notable achievement in the process of the promotion of modern system of education. After this the people of the state began to witness the degree of the increasing number of students who passed in other professional courses also. In 1914-15 Dr. Goberdhon Singh became the first medical graduate and in the year 1916-17 Shri Khomdram Angangjao Singh became the first Manipuri engineering graduate from the Dacca University. In the year 1918 the number of medical graduates had increased to three. The in the year 1922-23 two students i.e. Shri S. Somorandro Singh and L. Iboongohal Singh passed B.A. In 1924-25 one student got certificate in veterinary science. In the same year one student Shri Nabakanta Singh got B.Sc. degree. He was the first student in Manipur who got B.Sc. degree and in the year 1931 one Sinam Krishnamohon Singh got M.A. degree from Dacca University. He was the first person who received M.A. degree in Manipur. Thus within a short period Manipur was able to witness a tremendous growth in the number of educated people. Gradually they began to play a major role in very aspect of the social, political and economic life of the state. At the beginning they started their activities by joining in the state service. Through their respective profession these groups of people made a successful attempt to bring a drastic change in the nature and outlook of the common people. Their only objective was to free the society from the feudal and colonial system of administration and to replace it by the principles of democratic institutions. So in order to translate their objective in reality they tried to give awareness for the growth of political consciousness among the people. In their efforts they were greatly influenced by the political activities of the Indian national liberation movement. From the activities of the Indian National Movement they have received an experienced about the importance of the spirit of nationalism for the maintenance of their distinctive historical identity. Thus the tremendous successful efforts for the promotion of the modern system of education had rendered a great help in the production of nationalistic spirit among the educated middle class people in Manipur. Consequently they began to take the leadership of the society. So with a single agenda to promote and foster the political, social, economic and cultural life of the society these group of people had played various types of role for the betterment of the society.

Nikhil Hindu Manipuri Mahasabha

The establishment of the Nikhil Hindu Manipuri Mahasabha as social and religious organisation was a great breakthrough in the ongoing process of the outlook of the common people. As it has already been mentioned above about the nature of the people right from the early period of time. Under the feudal social system the people were not able to expand their horizon of vision and the growing mindset of the people were put under control by one way or other. Therefore under this prevailing situation the people were not able to raise their logical and rational voice for the betterment of the society. Such type of artificial restrictions made by the privileged section of the society was demolished by the educated middle class people with the establishment of this organisation. No doubt it was not a political organisation and there was no concrete political agenda in the objective. From the nature of the working style of the organisation it is quite evident that the only objective of the organizer was to bring all the elite section of the society to bring together under the banner of a single platform. Even the feudal ruler, Manipur was brought within the framework of this organisation. Such type of arrangement was indeed a highly mature game plan of the educated middle class people of this state. Thus from the year 1934 the activities of the organisation which asked for the maintenance of the unity among the Manipuris scattered the different area outside Manipur was carried on very effectively. At the same time they also used this platform as a means to give awareness among the people about the prevailing social, political, economic and cultural conditions which were developed in other parts of the globe.

Nikhil Manipuri Mahasabha

The establishment of this organisation as a political party was a notable achievement for all the people of the educated middle class who had already sharpened their mind with the idea of the spirit of Manipuri nationalism. It was established in the year 1938. On the other hand, the outbreak of such type of new phenomenon may be treated as an open ideological revolt of the middle class section of the society against the feudal system of administration. This political organisation was established by the same people who took great initiative for the establishment of Nikhil Hindu Manipur Mahasabha as a social and religious organisation. From this fact it is also observed that this social and religious organisation was a nucleus of the birth of political organisation in Manipur. The demand of the establishment of responsible government in Manipur based on the principle of democracy was a great threat to the existence of the feudal system of administration in the state. The educated people like Hijam Irabot Singh, Bankabehari Sharma, Lalita Madhop Sharma, Rajkumar Bhubonsana etc played a leading role in such great political venture. The demand for the abolition of kingship and establishment of people's government had produced a wonderful impact in the social and political life of the state. Now people also began to realise the immediate need to change the political and social landscape for the betterment of the people. Along with this political agenda the idea of Manipuri nationalism was also gaining its momentum in the mindset of the people under the leadership of the educated middle class have started to launch a non-violent type of political movement for the establishment of democratic institution. Such type of development was a great contribution of the leadership of educated middle class of the society.

Religious Revitalization movement

Apart from the political and social activities, the members of this group of people also actively played a great role in the movement to remind the people of their religion before the coming of Hinduism. Right from the beginning of the 18th century the influence of Hinduism began to enter into Manipur and subsequently this religion became a state religion. As a result of this the whole nature and mindset of the people was drastically changed from the traditional religious concept and practices. But with the emergence of new outlook in the mindset of the people particularly on the question of the promotion and maintenance of the distinctive historical identity of the place, the people of new generation who acquired the knowledge of modern education had strongly prepared to revitalize the primal religion and its practices of the state. They shortly believed that the revitalization of the traditional religion was also a very important issue in the process of the preservation of the national identity of Manipur. The establishment of Apokpa Marup under the leadership of Naoria Phullo as a very good platform for the religious revitalization movement and formation of 'Meetei Marup' as a social and religious organisation with basic objective to launch a mass involvement movement against the Hindu religion was also another notable contribution of these group of people.

Participation in the Movement for Responsible Government

Just after the emergence of Nikhil Manipuri Mahasabha as the political organisation the people began to witness the growth of other political parties who strongly asserted for the establishment of responsible government in Manipur. The idea of the establishment of a democratic principle in the administration of the state was the brain child of these groups of people. It has already been mentioned above about the strong intention of the group of middle class people in the system of the administration of the state. So, with the role objective to remove the feudal and colonial administration system they began to involve with a strong impetus for the establishment of responsible government. It was mainly because of their logical and rational political stand that the people were able to witness a new political setup in Manipur just after the departure of the colonial administration. The establishment of constitutional monarchical system was a significant change in the whole administrative set-up of the state. Along with this new political development the period of feudal system was also removed from the whole social life of the state. This is a democratic contribution of the people of educated middle class.

Statehood Movement and Growth of Separatist Idea

The most peculiar character of the educated middle class elements in the society of Manipur was their firm stand for having a distinctive historical identity of the people of the state. It is a well known fact that there was a sharp difference of opinion among the political leadership of the state on the issue of the integration of Manipur into India. Finally the pro-integration group of this section was able to take Manipur inside the political boundary of India in October 1949 with the hope that Manipur would become a prosperous state as a part and parcel of India. When it came out in reality the political outcome was against their high expectation. Then the same group of people who strongly asserted for integration of Manipur into India had started to express their resentment against the partial policy of India. Then by using their political platform, they started to launch a mass involvement movement in a non-violent way. This movement was popularly known as statehood movement. And it was continued for about two decades. Only in the year 1972, that too after having a continuous and consistent non-violent agitation, the long standing demand of the people was fulfilled. Thus Manipur became a full-fledged state of India. This was a major political achievement of the leadership of educated middle class.

Growth of the Separatist Tendency among the People

Apart from their non-violent type of political movement a section of the ultra elements among the educated middle section of the society have started to launch a violent type of movement with an objective to establish a distinctive identity of the people of the Manipur outside the boundary of the Indian Union. The idea was formulated in the middle of nineteen sixties when the political status of Manipur was not to the desire of the people these group of educated people who believed that the identity of the people of Manipur would completely become extinct if it continue to live inside the political boundary of the Indian Union. Therefore they felt that it could be possible only when some kind of violent type of movement had landed. On the basis of this belief they formed an armed organisation with some ideological touch and through this platform they made a serious attempt to carry the masses in favour of their objective.

Thus the educated middle class of the society played a very important role in the changing political scenario of the state. They had started their contribution by imparting knowledge of the importance of democratic principle against the feudal and colonial system. The establishment of responsible government on the basis of adult universal franchise was a major achievement of their effort. Therefore establishment of a popular government on the basis of democratic practice and to create an atmosphere for the growth of the idea of Manipuri nationalism may be treated as an outstanding contribution of these groups although people failed to see clearly the point of middle class.

NOTES

1. *Dictionary of Philosophy,* Progress Publishers 1984 V.I. Lenin, p. 68.
2. *Collected Works of Lenin,* Moscow, Vol. 29, p.421.
3. V.M. Dandekar, *Nature of Class Conflict in Indian Society*, 1978.
4. Karl Marx, *Theories of Surplus Value,* Part II 1975, p.573 quoted in *A Dictionary of Social Communism*, p. 135.
5. *A Dictionary of Social Communism*, Progress Publisher, 1980, p.135
6. B.B. Misra, *The Indian Middle Classes, Their growth in Modern Times*, 1961, p.VII.
7. *Ibid.* p.149.
8. Manipur Under British Management (1891-1906), Shillong.
9. Thokchom Mangoljao Singh, *Manipurda Nongchuplomgi Siksha*, Vol. I and II, 1989, p.3. (Western Education in Manipur in Manipuri), Imphal
10. *Ibid,* p. 5.
11. *Ibid,* p. 6.

5

THE CHANGING NATURE AND ROLE OF MIDDLE CLASS IN MANIPUR

Kshetri Bimola

The concept of middle class has been applied and interpreted in various contexts and in different directions. But there is a common agreement that the middle class play an important role in the growth and development of a given society, old and new. It was Aristotle who said that "the best community is formed by citizens of the middle class and that those states are likely to be well administered in which the middle class is large". The size and composition of the middle class may differ from society to society; primitive, traditional, agricultural, industrial, post-industrial and modern democratic ones. In the primitive society, those who exercised their minds and developed ideas for the regulation of the social and economic life may be termed as middle class. In a traditional society where chief-tains or rulers of small villages and kingdoms those who were near the position and political power, who had easy access to the political authority may be described as middle class. The size of the middle class got expanded in the agricultural society as it includes both the economically sound persons as well as those who had free access to the political power. The middle class in the agricultural society may include both the few groups of persons who are in the reign of administration as well as those who emerge themselves as economically sound persons by using their skill for more production having the control of resources, having the knowledge for taking advantages in the socioeconomic situation of the society. Both these groups are instrumental in the socioeconomic and political changes of the society. These old group of middle class in course of time, took a new form of middle class due to the emergence of the industrial society particularly in the western societies. The size of the middle class got expanded by consisting many groups, the traditionally having sound financial background, those persons who have acted as a link between the ruled and the ruler, the new group of employers in the industrial sector etc. This phase of middle class was particularly experienced in the nineteenth century Western Europe. In the 20th century with the democratization process taking root in many countries of the world, the middle class had started to play an important role in the economic and political life of the society. Starting from developed countries, the newly emerged middle class in the developing countries had played their role in shaping the policies and programmes of the state, indirectly influencing with their position and status in the society. The nature and the role of the middle class got changed with the process of globalization, privatization and liberalisation since the later part of the 20th century.

On the basis of the changing scenario of the middle class through different stages, an attempt is made to study the changing nature and role of the middle class in Manipur.

Middle Class during Pre-British Period

The modern concept of middle class having values, educational attainments, service sector employment could not be applied in the Manipuri society during the pre-British period. Manipur had monarchical form of government, the king as the head of the political authority having sovereign power. He was assisted by a group of ministers called Phamdous. There were 64 Phamdous representing 32 administrative divisions of the state. Of these 64 phamdous about ten were the core group like the present cabinet ministers in a parliamentary form of government. When we asked, who were the middle class these phamdous may be called the upper middle class linking the higher political authority and the people. The beauty of the system was that these groups of middle class were the representatives of their own administrative divisions.

But this positive feature of the middle class had disappeared slowly when the king exercised his supremacy in the appointment of his close relatives and favourites as ministers. This trend one finds in the later stage of monarchy in Manipur.

In addition to Phamdous, the close relatives of the king and favourites may also be included in the middle class category. Because it is these groups who enjoyed the social status by enjoying patronage and favour from the king. Regarding their role, it may be said that they only discharged those duties and responsibilities as assigned by the king from time to time. Sometimes they were also responsible for creating dissensions, conflicts, ill feelings etc. among the royal circle with an aim to topple down the rule of one king and install another to the supreme political authority.

After the establishment of the Political Agency in 1835 in Manipur, the nature of the middle class at the political level had undergone changes. The upper middle class namely the ministers had most of the time, acted independently of the Raja. "The minister and the officials, who preyed upon the people, publicly robbed them and presented their earning an honest livelihood".[1] These group of middle class did not encourage any innovation in the state, thinking that the changes would deprive them of the benefits and the advantages acquired by them. These changes in the nature and role of the middle class can be seen in Manipur in the late 19th century.

The land which belonged to the Raja was subdivided into villages. The headman of each division or village looked after the cultivation. The headman was the tax collector in kind by each cultivator. There were also grants of land by the Maharaja to officials and favourites. Relatives of the Raja, Brahmins and sepoys paid no rent or tax on their fixed proportion of land. These groups of middle class had enjoyed many privileges against the interest and welfare of the common people. The Political Agent Col. Johnstone observed that the Maharaja, Chandrakirti had left the administration including the judicial ones in the hands of favourites, friends and officers. The Maharaja trusted his advisors and high officials too much. Dr. R. Brown also had recorded that 2 baskets of paddy was nominally taken from the favourites and from others 12 baskets yearly. When middleman such as officials were involved, as high as 24 baskets by Pari were taken. This in one sense may be termed as extortion by the middle class. Every major or high official had taken what he wanted. This was rather justified on the ground that no salary was paid to the officials.

Middle Class during the British Period

After the establishment of political power in April, 1891, the British Political Agent Major St. P. Maxwell announced the abolition of Lallup system on 29th April, 1892. For the purpose of collecting land revenue, the valley was divided into 4 divisions or Panas, each under an officer called Lakpa. The four Panas namely Ahallup, Naharup, Laipham and Khabam were under the 4 Panas. In the appointment of Lakpas, the capacity of the men to be appointed as Lakpas in discharging the duties and responsibilities was not considered very important, rather given secondary importance. Men of influence and high social standing was given more importance by the appointing authority. To check the assessment of landtax and to measure land, 8 Amins were also appointed. These Lakpas and Amins, the newly emerging middle class were able to earn large amount of income by exerting the position and responsibilities assigned to them. It has been observed that the income of the Lakpas must be large than that of the most highly paid sub-deputy collector who was appointed in charge of the land revenue administration in August, 1897. To quote Maxwell, "the Manipuris with few exceptions cannot be trusted in positions of authority, and more especially in positions which entail the collection of public monies . . . time, education and example will, I hope, effect the change which we desire."[2] The collecting officers of revenue namely the Lakpas, the Kanungos and the Amins had opportunities of embezzlement and misappropriation of the revenue amount. Many irregularities were detected. There were cases of dismissal and resignation of Amins and Lakpas on account of misappropriation of state money, Later on, in the appointment of Amins and Lakpas, the knowledge and skill of a person and at the same time belonging to a respectable family was considered as most important.

On the other hand, the traditional middle class, the Brahmins and the Rajkumars had enjoyed privileges relating to land. Both these groups of middle classes were given rent free land and no part of the produce was given to loyal granaries while others had to pay. The Brahmins were exceedingly well off may be because of their priestly profession and temple worship.

The number of Rajkumars was increasing, might be due to the polygamy practiced by the Maharaja. When the Rajkumars had enjoyed rent free land, the Political Agent had suggested that both the Brahmins and the Rajkumars might be assessed at half rates. When Patta was issued under the supervision of the Sub-Deputer Collector there was protest from Rajkumars.

Regarding the cause of the first Nupilan 1904, the Political Agent and the British officers believed that the middle class, the Brahmins and the Rajkumars were responsible for raising the womenfolk against the British. These middle class had never loyally accepted the order of the Political Agent to rebuild the house of the Asstt. Political Agent. The burning of the house was only an instance where by a side issue, they could express their great dislike to the order of the paramount power[3]. The Brahmins were also charged for inducing the womenfolk not to attend the markets. In the given situation, it was the lower middle class i,e the newly appointed members of the Cheirap and the Panchayat courts, chawkidars etc. who were in between the British authority and the traditional upper middle class mainly the Rajkumars. These classes were asked to implement the orders of the Political Agent on one hand and on the other the Rajkumars asked them to disobey the orders.

In 1919 when there was increase in the price of rice quite high than normal, the Political Agent C. Gimson in his report mentioned that it was the middle class who suffered most[4]. There was remarkable high price of rice in 1921 and there was extra ordinary increase in the number of dacoities committed in the richer men's godowns. The richer section of the population was targeted from 2 sides i.e, the British authority and the poor people. It is noteworthy to mention that very few Manipuri Hindus appeared at the poor asylums. This was probably due to the fact that in many cases the richer men in the village were constrained by the force of public opinion or by fear of being looted, to support the poorer inhabitants by loans of paddy. Several cases of forced loans from those who had large stocks of paddy were reported, but there was no widespread agitation.[5]

The beginning of 1930s was marked by a new trend in the role of middle class led by persons who received education from outside the state. Their role was in two directions, one, joining the governmental authority and the other by taking up steps to awaken the minds of the people towards democratic directions. Among the educated persons who had joined the Manipur State Darbar were (1) S. Somarendra Singh, B.A., (2) H. Dwijamani Sarma, M.A., (3) L. Ibungohal Singh, B.A. LLB, and (4) S. Nadia Singh, B.A. The other State officials were (1) H. Irabot Singh, Member, Sadar Panchayat Court, (2) A. Dorendrajit Singh, B.A., (3) Ch. Pishak Singh, M.A, (4) Atombapu Sarma, (5) Lalita Madhab Chatterjee, (6) M. Madhumangol Singh, (7) Sinam Krisha Mohan Singh, M.A, B.L., and (8) Angom Janaki Nath. "A Western educated class, torn between seeking their identity in a cultural renaissance and wanting a share in political and economic power was beginning to emerge."[6]

The then prevailing socio-religious situation exploited by „Brahma Sabha forcefully implementing the practice of Mangba Sengba in the name of religion had given rise to the assertion of anti authority attitude and outlook in the mind of the educated middle class. The three, namely the Maharaja, the Brahma Sabha (Council of Brahamins) and the Ratan were responsible for declaring any person/persons, family or villages to be untouchables (mangba), Socially boycotted/outcasted, not allowing to cremate even the dead body according to vaishnavite religion. The untouchables (Mangba) or polluted could again become sengba (unpolluted) by paying money to the Ratan, Brahma Sabha and the Maharaja.

The new educated middle class made a shrewd move by establishing the Nikhil Hindu Manipuri Mahasabha with the Maharaja as president and Hijam Irawat as vice president on 30th May, 1934. Later on this new group of middle class moved on two different directions, (1) Pro-authority middle class sharing the position and power in the administrative hierarchy enjoying higher social status and (2) the other strruggling on behalf of the common people in the midst of the Brahmin dominated society. Irawat along with his friends Bankabihari Sharma, Lalita Madhab Sarma, Kanhai, Longjam Bijoy started to take up activities against the Mangba-Sengba practices. Irawat went from village to village and cremated the dead bodies from the graves and performed potloiba in the Vaishanvite tradition. Irawat also performed the shradha ceremonies, himself taking the role of Ishei Hanba (the leader of the group of singers). Irawat may be called the real leader of the middle class group fighting against the oppressive and the exploitative system of Mangba Sengba and making the common people aware of the then autocratic and authoritative political system. To accommodate the non-Hindus, Irawat was instrumental in deleting the word "Hindu" from Nikhil Hindu Manipuri Mahashbha at the fourth session held at Chinga in 1938 on 29 and 30 December. It was also in this session that the Nilkhil Manipur Mahasabha was declared as the first political party of Manipur. The importance and significance of the Chinga session of the Mahasabha lies in the fact that the demand for democratic political system emerged for the first time in Manipur in the form of resolutions.

The emergence of the new educated middle class with a democratic mind since 1930s marked a very important phase in political history of Manipur. The modern concept of middle class as educated, hard working and patient may rightly be applied to them.

The immediate cause for the outbreak of the second Nupilan (Women's movement), 1939 was due to the scarcity of rice in the main market, Khwairamband Bazar, Imphal. Though it was essentially a women's movement, Irawat and his friends had guided and given new ideas and initiatives for the emergence of democratic ideas among the womenfolk as well as the people of Manipur at large in the later stage of the movement. The demand for full responsible government, adult franchise, legislature etc. in the later 1940s were the after effects of the ideas and activities of the middle class led by Irawat.

Middle Class in Manipur, 1947-1972

After getting independence on 15th August, 1947, the leading personalities of Manipur to be designated as middle class were all busy in the changing political scenario of Manipur, from a monarchical system to the democratic system under the Manipur State Constitution Act, 1947. Many of them were interested in the participation in the electoral politics and to get themselves elected to the Manipur State Legislative Assembly.

When the general elections for parliament and electoral college were held in 1952, the middle class group had given their attention to the elections, more to the electoral college. They might have thought that this electoral college will play an important role in the politics of the state. The ethnic based partics and the large number local parties putting up their own candidates in the elections shows this trend. Another section of educated middle class had entered the government service and found themselves satisfied, enjoying higher social status and financial stability. When the electoral college consisting of 30 elected members was dissolved after electing Lalita Madhab Sharma as an M.P. to the Council of States (Rajya Sabha), the only political gain was the raising of political awareness and consciousness in the mind of the people, mainly the middle class group. On the other hand, the number of educated youths attending college from the middle class group also increased and it ultimately helped in demanding the restoration of responsible government, 1948 in the middle of 1950s; a legislature in the early 1960s and in demanding the fullfledged status of Manipur in late 1960s within the Indian Union. The educated middle class group, both in the government service as well as in the socio-political fields had dominated the changing scenario of Manipur during the period, 1947 to 1972.

Middle Class in Manipur, 1972-1980

The short period of 8 years from 1972-1980 may be described to be a striking phase in the growth of new middle class based on income. Manipur after attaining full fledged status within the Indian Union was entitled to exercise legislative, executive and financial powers given in the Constitution of India. The enjoyment of these powers had given rise to the emergence of a new middle class namely the engineers and the contractors. The politicians including the ruling and the opposition[7] very often had to depend on the engineers and the contractors for their financial support. The higher social and financial status of the engineers and the contractors was recognized by the society. Even the farmers having small amount of capital were attracted towards the work of the contractors. There was a saying that "what is the use of wasting time in the cultivation when one can earn a lot in contract work . In the marriage market, the parents of highly educated girl, a post graduate, preferred a contractor for the marriage of their daughter. It was also a common talk among the girls studying post-graduate in the University about the contractors. The engineers and the contractors always go together. So the 1970s was the time of the engineers and the contractors dominating the social and the economic scene of Manipur. There was a handloom silk Innafi (chaddar) a very costly one called Engineer s Innafi. On further inquiry, it is found that only the wives of the engineers could buy the costly silk Innafi. This clearly shows that the fruits of the economic empowerment of Manipur indirectly helped some persons to grow financially to enroll themselves as new category of middle class in Manipur.

The educated middle class had increased its number due to the establishment of the Centre for Post Graduate Studies, Imphal under the Jawaharlal Nehru University, New Delhi. Many also received their education at a higher level; general, professional and technical from other Universities, professional Institutions etc. But this educated middle class could not play a creative role in the society, might be due to their learning stage of the society, not possessing applicable knowledge. In brief it may be summed up by saying that the people including the middle class were quite happy at the attainment of statehood where fruits were shared by the politicians, the engineers and the contractors.

Middle Class in Manipur since 1980

The social scenario of Manipur in the 1980s was marked by an undesired, anti-social features affecting the normal atmosphere of the life of the people. Due to the growth of insurgent organizations in the late 1970s, the beginning of 1980 had given rise to the conflict between the central security forces and the insurgents. The imposition of the Armed Forces Special Power Act, 1958 in September, 1980 and consequent arrests, enforced dis-appearance of persons, rape, molestation, sexual abuse, killings etc. had led to a very unstable society affecting the economy of the state. The common people could not concentrate on their normal agricultural and other occupational activities. The high degree of social instability caused by the armed conflict between the security personnel and the insurgents had dominated the society of Manipur. To protect the menfolk particularly the youths, the womenfolk of Manipur came out from their homes and started to guard their localities from the security personnel with torches in their hands in the night. These women came to be known as Meira Paibis.

The year 1980 is also important when we traced the history of the growth of higher education in Manipur. The Manipur University was established in 1980 as the higher educational institution in the state by an agreement between the authority of Jawaharlal Nehru University and the Government of Manipur for taking over the erstwhile Centre for Post Graduate Studies, Imphal and merged it into Manipur University. The Centre for Post Graduate Studies had already produced students with post graduate degrees during the period of eight years w.e. from 1972 to 1980. This small section of the educated middle class could not bring change in the society. But with the establishment of Manipur University, the teachers as well as the students had started to study critically the socio-political and economic history of Manipur. The research activities taken up by the teachers and the students greatly helped in unfolding many areas of the socio-political history of Manipur in relation with the British authority and subsequent merger of Manipur into the Indian Union.

The two decades i.e. 1980s and 1990s may be described as the re-awakening period of the people of Manipur. It was during this period that some of the teachers had contributed their intellectual ideas in understanding the past socio-economic and political happenings and the impact on the present day society of Manipur. Large member of awareness programmes in the form of symposiums, workshops, seminars, conferences etc. were organized by the local clubs, non-governmental organizations (NGOs) and voluntary organizations etc. on the various aspects of Manipur by inviting University teachers and other resource persons. As a result of these interactions, even ordinary men and women came to know about the Manipur Merger Agreement, 1949, the Armed Forces Special Power Act, 1958, the political system of India and the status of Manipur as a federating Unit within the Indian Union. The highly educated middle class from the

University and others had contributed in reawakening the people Manipur, mainly the youths though suffered due to the armed conflict situation prevailing in the state.

The beginning of the 21st century had witnessed the development of an important issue affecting the territorial integrity of Manipur. The conclusion of the Ceasefire Agreement between the Government of India and the Nationalist Socialist Council of Nagaland (NSCN-IM) in June 2001 had created a very alarming situation in the mind of the people of Manipur. The inclusion of the terms "without territorial limits"in the Indo-Naga Ceasefire Agreement had been interpreted so as to include the Naga inhabited Areas of Manipur, Assam and Arunachal Pradesh in the proposed "Nagalim" by NSCN (I-M). The people of Manipur became unrest and general strike was called continuously for 3 days affecting the lives of the people. Sensing strong reaction from the people in the form of movement, the government of Manipur had imposed curfew, not allowing the people to come out from home. Inspite of the curfew imposed by the government, people in large numbers, namely the womenfolk had organized sit-in protest in different areas of Manipur. The educated middle class who had deep knowledge of the history of the Nagas of Manipur and their relationship with the valley people had spoken in these sit-in-protests cum meetings organized by clubs/Associations and voluntary organizations. It is worthy to note that not a single instance of violence happened between the Nagas and the valley people though the tension was quite high between the two sections of the population. It was only in July 27, 2001 that the Government of India had announced the deletion of the term "without territorial limits" from the Indo-Naga ceasefire Agreement.

The social scene of Manipur from 2001 to 2009 was full of complicated issues i.e, the negotiation between the Government of India and the NSCN (IM), the latter demanding the inclusion of the Naga inhabited areas of Manipur for the creation of Nagalim; the armed conflict situation between the Security personnel and the insurgents; the violation of human rights (the killing of Manorama, 2004 being a leading case); the assertion of ethnic identities by the Nagas and the Kukis; the shooting down of youths by the State Security Personnel (the Commandos) and the formation of Joint Action Committee in each case of shooting of a youth etc. It may be said that the Manipur society was in turmoil, full of complicated issues affecting the general interest of the people. The kidnapping of persons for ransoms, planting of bombs, grenades at the residences of bureaucrats, pradhans, chairpersons of local bodies like Zillah Parishads, Municipal Councils had added another dimension in the prevailing conflict situation in Manipur. On the government side, the recruitment of police forces at the level of Sub-Inspectors, Assistant Sub-Inspectors, constables etc. was another step taken up in order to control the law and order situation. Economic blockades, bandhs, general strikes called by various different organizations in the last 2 decades were another dimension affecting the economy of the state resulting in the increase of prices in the essential commodities.

In the midst of these social instability, social conflicts and political conflicts, there emerged a different group of middle class based on income. These new middle class consists of contractors, businessmen, persons who had easy access to the administrative and political authority, the black marketeers dealing with drugs, small arms etc. There seems to be a clash of interests and competition between the two groups of middle class i.e the educated middle class and the newly emerged middle class based on income. The latter was very forceful and assertive that the Manipur society was dominated by this class to some extent in the last 2 decades. Of course it is often said that the fruit in the conflict situation is usually enjoyed by persons who are in authority and persons who are close to the authority. In the name of insurgency, the funds meant to utilize for the control of insurgency and for the maintenance of law and order had given an opportunity to some sections of middle class to grow richer and thereby raise their status in the society.

The assertion of ethnic identity by some major tribes of Manipur had indirectly helped the new middle class who are in administrative position and political authority to earn more income by taking advantages of the economic blockade called by the Nagas and the Kukis. Mention may be made of economic blockade called by United Naga Council (UNC), All Naga Students Union, Manipur (ANSUM) for 65 days in 2010; economic blockade for 120 days in 2011 called by both Sadar Hills District Demand Committee (Kuki) and by the United Naga Council.

The two national highways No.2 (earlier No.39) and No. 37 (earler No. 53) are the only two routes connecting Manipur with other states like Nagaland and Assam. The essential commodities are brought to Manipur only through these 2 routes. During the period of economic blockades, the prices of essential commodities had increased beyond the capacity of the common people. One gas cylinder costs above Rs. 2000/- one litre of petrol more than Rs. 200/-; one kilo of potato Rs. 30/-; one kilo of sugar Rs. 50/-etc. In the given situation, we may classify middle class in two groups, one who are in advantageous position by involving in the black marketeering in selling gas cylinders, petrols etc. at a higher rate, thus earning extra income. Another group of middle class, mainly in the autonomous and educational institutions facing hardships in procuring gas cylinders and petrols etc. They had to buy these essential items at a higher price form the black marketeers. The size of the second group of middle class in small and had to bear the burden of the rising prices.

Thus the middle class is found to be divided in their nature and role in the Manipuri society as majority are always working in their own interests. This may be the reason for the silence of the people though faced economic hardship due to economic blockade in 2011. In answering questions in press conference in New Delhi on 31st October, 2011, the Home Minister P. Chidambaram said that "The peculiar feature of this blockade is, although the valley especially Imphal is affected, there are no protest in Imphal as such"[8] People are facing hardship due to economic blockade,. The reason for not having protest against the economic blockade might be the promotion of self interest of a section of middle class who were involved in earning extra income.

It is a fact that the size of the middle class is expanding in due course of time e.g. the sudden increase of large number of small vehicles including the costly ones and the number of RCC multi storeyed buildings coming up in and around Imphal area. Chief Minister, O. Ibobi had expressed on two occasins in 2011 that government will take up steps to trace the source of income of the persons having costly cars and multi-storeyed buildings.

On the whole when we study the nature and the role of middle class since pre-British days in Manipur, it is found that the middle class had changed in accordance with the changing situation and the nature of the political authority from time to time. During the pre-british period, it was the nobilities, the relatives and friend circle of the Monarch who exercised the dominating role by taking advantage of the political power and position. The composition and the role of the middle class had changed with the coming of the British from 1891 to 1947, including those who were recruited by the British administration namely the Lakpas, the Amins, the Kanungos as well as the educated ones who became the members of the Darbars. The members of the Mahasabha exercising religious control over the people in the name of Mangba-Sengba had played a negative role trying to promote their self interest. The newly educated middle class emerged with a strong social and political force since 1947. They had played their role in a positive and creative manner in the interest of the people and society at large. Through the size of the middle class mainly the educated ones employed in government services had increased tremendously, their role is only to promote their self interest while discharging their duties. Another section of the middle class working in autonomous institutions are not able to assert themselves giving new ideas, may be because of the conflict situation prevailing in Manipur since 1980. The autonomous middle class emerged in the conflict situation, raising their income tremendously instead of serving the society with their ideas, have worked in the opposite direction promoting corruption on a large scale. Thus the concept of middle class promoting values, cultural affinities, creative atmosphere in the society with their new ideas is applicable only in a very limited degree in Manipur. The present day middle class (majority) in Manipur believe in "rewards without efforts" and rights without responsibilities.

NOTES AND REFERENCES

1. K. Manimohan Singh, *NUPILAL (Women's War of Manipur)*, K. Premlata Devi, Imphal, 2000, p.3-4.
2. H. St.P. Maxwell, *Administration Report of the Political Agency*, Manipur, 1898-99, No.70, p. 7.
3. *Ibid.*

4. C. Gimson, ICS, *Administration Report of the Manipur State for the Year, 1919-20*, Imphal, p.9.
5. C.S. Mullan, M.A., ICS, President, Manipur State Darbar, Administration Report of Manipur State, 1921-22, Imphal, p.11.
6. Parratt, John, *Wounded Land*, Mittal Publications, New Delhi, 2005, p.23.
7. During the period 1972 to 1977, there were as many as six ministries due to rampant defection of elected MLAs. There was maximum degree of ministerial instability.
8. *The Hindu,* 1st November, 2011.

6

MIDDLE CLASS POLITICS IN POST-COLONIAL MANIPUR (1950-1972)

N. Lokendra Singh

The sudden integration of Manipur into the Indian Union in October 1949 led to significant changes in the political structure of the princely state as well as its relation with the Indian Union. The economy of the state had also been undergoing significant changes since World War II. As the forces of the post-Independence market economy had penetrated into the peripheral areas, the earlier poise, calm and general euphoria had begun to be rudely shaken. At another level the hopes and aspirations of many leaders of the valley based Manipuri middle class, were absolutely belied by the eroded status and power of a part 'C' state coupled with their inability to fit into the new structures of the society. Indeed the new arrangement could not provide sufficient avenues of either democratizing the political system of the state or accommodating the educated middle class in the higher echelons of the power structure. It was in such a situation of complex socio-economic and political reality that the Manipuri middle class, particularly the valley based group, which had undertaken prolonged anti-colonial and anti-feudal struggle (1934-1949) became deeply polarised into three main political groups i.e., Manipur State Congress (MSC), Manipur Communist Party (MCP) and the Socialist Party (SP).[1] Most of the important leaders of these parties were urban based but with landed backgrounds. Praja Shanti a short lived political party consisting of amorphous groups which emerged in 1948 under the protection of the then Maharaja Bodhachandra Singh continued to be involved in state politics till the 1950's. The Party however did not have any clear cut political ideology and as a result it had gone into insignificance after about 6-7 years of its existence.

There were a lot of political realignments in Manipur hills too. While the British Indian Govt. was toying with the idea of 'Crown Colony' comprising the hill areas of northeast India and upper Burma, on the eve of India's independence, there was a process of ethnic consolidation in Manipur. The missionary educated middle class of Manipur hills who were exposed to the different political cross currents during the War began to form numerous ethnic organizations like the 'Kabui Naga Association'(KNA), 'Tangkhul Long'(TL), 'Kuki National Assembly'(KNA), 'Hmar National Union'(HNU), 'Paite National Council'(PNC) etc. These different groups were also trying to respond to the rapidly changing political scenario in the state as well as at the National level. Indeed, for the first time in their long history of struggle for survival and also against British colonialism and feudal rule, the hill people were given the opportunity of participating in the struggle for democratization of politics in Manipur as well as other forms of ethnocentric political processes. As will be subsequently seen, the hopes and aspirations of the educated middle class were exhibited in the entire gamut of their political activities.

II

POLITICAL STRUCTURE OF A PART-C STATE

With effect from the 15th October 1949, Manipur was integrated into the Indian union and the administration of the State was handed over to the 1st Chief Commissioner designate, Rawal Amar Singh.[2] Along with it the power and authority of the Maharaja which was mandated under the Manipur Constitution Act 1947 stood withdrawn.[3] The 53 member Legislature along with the Council of Ministers which were established in 1948 were immediately dissolved. For reasons known only to the Govt. of

India the new Chief Commissioner was replaced by Himat Singh K Maheshwari in November itself. With the enforcement of the constitution of India on 26th January 1950, Manipur was given the constitutional status of a Part-C State of Indian union. The Govt. of India vested enormous executive and judicial power to the Chief Commissioner. The Chief Commissioner "may appoint such judges , magistrates and the other officers as may be necessary for the administration of Manipur and may by general or special order determine their jurisdiction powers ,duties, and functions"[4] subject to the control of the central govt. The President of India was to constitute an Advisory Council consisting of the Chief Commissioner and 14 other members to be nominated by the central Govt. in consultation with the Chief Commissioner. The Chief Commissioner was the head of the Administration and he was assisted by a Secretariat with a Chief Secretary and six other Secretaries, two of whom are ex-officio Secretaries and other ancillary officers.[5] The state was administered as a single district territory. P.C. Dev a former land revenue officer during the native rule was hurriedly appointed the 1st Assistant to the Chief Commissioner which was subsequently redesignated as Chief Secretary relegating H. Birahari Singh and Th.Kalachand Singh, both local men to the rank of the 2nd and 3rd Assistant respectively. M.N. Phukan who hailed from the neighbouring state of Assam was also appointed as District Commissioner and K.C.Chakraborty as the Legal Remembrancer. Among the local politicians R.K.Maipaksana Singh was appointed as the Publicity Officer because of his consistent support for abolition of the kingship, only to resign from the coveted post in 1950 to start a new political party i.e. Manipur National Union.[6]

On matters related with law & order problem during the 1950's the state was administered as one Police District. Shri Palit who hailed from the neighbouring state of Bengal was appointed as the Superintendent of Police and he was assisted by L. Gopal Singh as the Assistant Superintendent of Police. The state police was organized in an expanded scale due to the serious law and order problem in the state. The number of recorded crimes increased from 831 in 1951-52 to 1050 in 1952-53.[7] In 1960 the sanctioned strength of the Civil Police constituted 1 Superintendent of Police, 9 Additional/Deputy Superintendent of

Police, 84 Inspectors/Sub-Inspectors, 157 Sergeants/Head Sergeants and 800 Foot Constables. Similarly, the State Military Police was also re-organized after the integration and formed the nucleus of the present Manipur Rifles. In 1961, the strength of the Manipur Rifles consisted 1 Commandant, 2 Assistant Commandant, 26 J.C.Os and 790 Rifle men.[8] The Police Department had also a regular C.I.D. branch and a police wireless grid covered a major portion of the Territory.

The state of the economy immediately after the merger was pretty disturbing. Out of a total amount of Rs.158.4 lakhs sanctioned during the First Five Year Plan only a sum of Rs.36.6 lakhs could be spent in development activities of the state due to recurrent agitations and civil disturbances. It may be interesting to note that six Chief Commissioners were appointed during a span of 8 years i.e.1949-1957. Although 92% of the cropped area which amounted to 2,23,034 acres grew paddy there were many instances of shortage of food crop in Manipur.[9] Manipur imported almost every item of daily consumption goods other than food crops i.e. petroleum, kerosene ,textiles and other manufactured goods. The supply of all these items was controlled by the outside traders who had their godowns and business shops at the lucrative Khwairamband Bazaar at Imphal. Altogether 44 marwari traders who fled from Manipur during the World War II were permitted to reoccupy their shop sites at Sadar Bazar, Maxwell Bazar and Muchipara which they had deserted during the war period under protection of the colonial officers during 1945-46.[10] Thus the pre-condition for a future subordination of the local businessmen to the outside traders were set. R.Constantine wrote that "the domination of non Manipuri business class" could be easily seen in the two main shopping centres of Imphal, Paona Bazar and Thangal Bazar.[11] An extremely unpopular practice of the local govt. during the 1950's was forcible 'procurement' of surplus paddy from the local farmers and export it out of the state in collusion with the Marwari traders. The state exported 2-3 lakh mds of parched rice in a normal year[12] which intermittently led to shortage of rice in the local market and thereby arousing popular protest against the outside traders.

A significant achievement of the state during the 1950's, however, was a tremendous expansion in the number of educational institutions as well as number of enrolled students. The number of primary schools had gone up from a mere 455 to a staggering figure of 1660 in 1961 whereas the number of secondary schools had increased from 82 in 1951 to 370 in 1961. The number of students enrolled in primary schools and secondary schools had gone up from 28896 to 106322 and 11642 to 48132 in 1951 and 1961 respectively. While the number of college in the state was only 1 in 1951 there were 5 colleges in 1961. The number of college students enrolled increased from 548 to 2014 in the corresponding years.[13] The result of such a trend of tremendous educational expansion against the back drop of economy of arrested production was "extreme unemployment and under employment in Manipur state.[14] E Kunjeshwar cautioned that "The persons in the helm of affair should consider the matter calmly and ways and means should be devised for improving the employment situation so that the educated young men may be saved from frustration and discouragement."[15]

III

THE STRUGGLE FOR POLITICAL DEMOCRATISATION IN MANIPUR

A. Anti-Chief Commissioner Agitation (1950-52)

Only after two months of his tenure as Chief Commissioner Rawal Amar Singh handed over the charge to his successor Himat Singh on 11th December 1949. Like his predecessor, Himat Singh due to his arbitrary nature of functioning as well as his attempt to encourage the Praja Shanti Party became unpopular among the conscious group of people in the state.

Meanwhile, the first Advisory Council was inaugurated on 9th October, 1950. It consisted of 14 members representing different parties like Praja Shanti, Manipur State Congress and some hill based parties with N. Ibomcha Singh of Praja Shanti Party as the Vice President. The Congress had 5 members in the Council. On the inaugural day, the Council under strong pressure from the Socialists party decided to withdraw the 'Permit System' which required any outsider attempting to enter Manipur to obtain an official permission from the competent authority.[16] During the colonial rule, the local authority had introduced the permit system in order to contain uncontrolled intrusion of Nepali grazers and outside traders in the state. In the second meeting of the Council which was held on 6th February 1951, the Congress members of the Council pressed the members to have a thorough discussion regarding the popular protest against scarcity of 'weavers yarn' in the market. As the Chief Commissioner was unwilling to initiate the discussion he walked out of the meeting after handing over the charges to N. Ibomcha Singh of Praja Shanti. The Congress members also subsequently walked out of the meeting. It may be important to note that in the 1950's nearly 50% of the population were given employment by handloom industry alone. In 1956 there were as many as 1,55,278 looms, of which 73,627 were loin looms, 64,949 were throw-shuttle looms and 11,702 were fly-shuttle looms.[17] Eventually all the Congress advisors left the Council on 12th February, 1951 under the directives of the party.[18]

Ch. Pishak Singh, one of the early educationists of the State assessed the performance of Himat Singh and wrote, "As a unifying factor, he ... miserably failed. He had carefully nursed a caucus of interested persons, the Praja Shanti, as a political body though it has no explicit policy and programme, though it does not maintain even the roll of register of its members."[19] Pishak Singh further wrote, "In nominating the members on the Advisory Council, he (gave) much more importance to Praja Shanti party then even to the State Congress as though the latter is the only major political party with backings of the major portion of the populace. The respective strengths of these two parties on the said council are seven and four".[20] Thus, the Chief Commissioner was accused to have "virtually created a party by making it loom large in the eyes of the ignorant public as a counter party set against the Congress".[21] Indeed, the leaders as well as active members of the State Congress was thoroughly disillusioned and frustrated with the new developments. The anger and frustration of the leaders of the Manipur State Congress was reflected in many of the editorials of the contemporary local newspapers. An editorial of *Janmabhumi* commented "A great wave of dissatisfaction and injured pride prevailed in the hearts of all Manipuris when the new Chief Commissioner had transformed the Administrative staffs ... when he did not give due consideration of the local people in his administrative reforms which he, with a very infant knowledge of the local people and situation had brought out without consulting any public leader or body".[22] It was further stated that "People are grudging against imposing Central Taxes when the benefits of the Central Govt. are not realized. The common people's lot has not been improved much but on the contrary has deteriorated since integration. Now therefore nothing short of responsible government with a Congress Chief Commissioner may satisfy the people of Manipur".[23] It was in such a situation that RK Jhalajit Singh a product of Calcutta University, a leader of State Congress had emphatically argued "non violent agitation had expedited the introduction of responsible self government (during 1947-1948)...despite the Maharaja's inertia ....if we wish to rejuvenate the political economic and social life of the people and thereby move to demand rightful place in independent India with our heads held high we should all be courageous. There is no place for conservatism in today's world and the future has to be decided by the revolutionary leaders".[24]

The State Congress having decided to confront the authority directly took the first step by way of organizing a "Chief Commissionergi sasan pamdabagi meeting" (meeting protesting against the Chief Commissioner's administration) at Gandhi Maidan on 25th February 1951. The meeting discussed the entire gamut of the popular grievances of the people under the new dispensation and decided to demand "poorna dayeetwashil shashan (responsible government)" in the state.[25] During the course of discussion the Congress strongly protested against the construction of an earthen Dam on the Imphal River as it led to scarcity of water downstream of the river. The Chief Commissioner clarified on the same day that water for villagers lower down the dam would be supplied by the Government and the dam was meant for flood prevention purposes.[26] In response, the Government tried to counter the move by organizing an exhibition for three weeks at the central square of Imphal i.e. Pologround as well as John stone School Campus. The government closed three high schools during the days of exhibition. There were large scale distribution of 'weavers yarns' to the hawkers of the exhibition. The Congress used the opportunity to expose the government by intensifying their opposition to the administration. The Congress scathingly attacked the government for disturbing the normal academic programme of the schools and also for clandestine distribution of yarns to some selected hawkers of the exhibition. Subsequently, the State Police raided Gandhi Maidan and arrested six active members of the Congress viz Ng. Tompok, L. Jugeshwor, P.Tomal, N. Birendra Kumar, N. Tomcha Sharma and M. Mani all belonging to the older generation of the State Congress sponsored exhibition was declared as illegal. A pamphlet entitled "Public discontent in exhibition" was hurriedly circulated by the members of the youth Congress including L.Joy Chandra Singh and N.Tombi Singh, on 4th March. It was strongly argued that the Govt. should not indulge in the practice of sabotaging any form of democratically organized meeting and the arrested Congress leaders should be immediately released. It was also stated that the artisans of the state should be given rent free stalls for exhibiting their products. When the Congress leaders were released on 5th March they were given a hero's welcome.

As the State Congress tried to reopen their exhibition on 11th March, the security forces immediately drove out the organizers and the place was cordoned off by the Manipur Rifles. Conversely, places within 1 miles radius of the Government sponsored Mela was put under 144 CRPC to avoid any form of disturbances. The security forces arrested eight cadres of the Congress on 15th March for attempting to defy and the prohibitory orders. The Congress workers were, however, not cowed down by such repressive measures. In an immediate move, on the next day, a more radical group within the Congress took a more proactive role by forming the "Gandhian Mela Karmi Sangh" and resolved to defy the prohibitory order. On the same day, 13 volunteers who came to Gandhi Maidan shouting slogans were arrested. On 17th March, 6 more senior leaders including L. Jugeshwor, P. Tomal Singh, K Kunjabihari Singh and Lalita Madhop Sharma, all were arrested.

The Socialist party led by L. Achou Singh and Rishang Keishing both products of Calcutta University also tried to fish in the ongoing unrest at Imphal. The SP had been trying to gain political mileage in the given situation. On 15th March 1951 itself the party organized a massive procession at the Imphal Bazaar defying the prohibitory orders of the government. The government arrested 68 persons who were mostly its sympathizers. In a pamphlet entitled "Praja pumnamakta haijaba (appeal to the people)" the party accused the Congress for colluding with the authority. While appealing to the people of Manipur in general and the community of teachers, clerks and peasants in particular to support the programme of the party, it was argued that due to rampant black marketeering, the Govt. could not distribute food items at controlled price[27]. In another pamphlet issued on 16th March the Party appealed to the people for supporting its programme of picketing the bazar on the same day against price rise[28]. Because of the intensified mass agitation, the government released all the arrested leaders of the Congress and Socialist party but with the understanding that the Presidents and General Secretaries of the two parties shall co-operate with the Government in rooting out black marketing in the supply of weavers yarn and other essential items. It further agreed upon that 144 CrPC should be immediately withdrawn from Imphal.

It was during such a politically charged situation that a section of the Congress leaders was trying to expand the base of their struggle by fomenting the agitation launched by the students of DM College demanding for withdrawal of the suspension order issued against S. Jayakishor Singh. Mr. Singh was alleged to have been involved in an accident in which a woman had died.[29] The students of the college constituted a 15 member Action committee with C. Upendra Singh as the leader. The committee had organized a meeting at Gandhi Maidan on 31st December to discuss the future course of action. The college authority tried to nib the movement in the bud by rusticating 3 student leaders i.e. Brajachand Singh, N. Tombi Singh and Chitreshwar Singh all of whom were active members of the State Congress. Two other students i.e. Upendra Singh, Singhajit Sana were suspended for one year and seven others were fined Rs.10 per head.[30] The students of the college responded by launching Satyagraha on 11 February 1952 at the college gate. The Govt. subsequently acted with a heavy hand by arresting 132 satyagrahis. Such high handed attitude of the authority further provoked the students' community and on 12th December they called a strike for the release of the students. The security forces used repressive measures to control the strikers. On 14th February when the students of the nearby Kha Imphal High School organized a rally demanding the release of the students from jail the state police forcibly stopped the rallyist. On the next day Hawaibam Tombi Singh and W. Kulabidhu Singh of the Socialist Party appealed to the student community of Manipur to go on strike from 16th February onwards as a mark of protest against the repressive measures adopted by the authority.[31] The Kwairamband Bazar at Imphal and some other smaller markets of the nearby villages like Thoubal, Awang Sekmai, etc were on hartal. Realising the gravity of the situation some of the senior Congress members including S.Krishna Mohan Singh and H.Dwijmani Sharma, senior leaders of the Congress intervened and convinced the students to come to the negotiating table. When the students met the Chief Commissioner Mr.E.P.Moon on 10th March 1952 they were told that there was no room for withdrawing the expulsion order.[32] The students still expressed their defiance by giving an ultimatum that if their demands including withdrawal of expulsion orders of the student and holding another test examinations for B.A. students would not be fulfilled in the next few days ,they would again resume the agitation.[33] On 3rd April about 5000 students went on a procession from Gandhi Maidan demanding for the removal of the college Principal[34]. A press note issued by thc state Govt. stated that the cases of the expelled students would be considered only if the strikers expressed regret and start attending classes regularly. It was also stated that the parents of the strikers should exercise influence upon their wards so that proper discipline could be observed in the college.[35] Despite this, the students continued their struggle. On 5th April the markets in and around Imphal were on hartal. They also blocked the movement of vehicles and passersby at Maharani and Chekthong bridge at the main Imphal market. As a result of such defying attitude about 15 activists were arrested and many others beaten up by the state police. Meanwhile the Governing body of the college had a meeting on 6th April with Maharaj Kumar P.B.Singh, the former Chief Minister, as the chairman and unanimously resolved that the punishment meted out to the students be withdrawn. Subsequently the strike was suspended on the same day.

The Manipur State Congress took opportunity to impress upon Pandit Nehru, the Prime Minister of India on matters related with the agitation in the state when he visited the state in October

1952. A memorandum dated 20th October 1952 inter alia included establishment of an Advisory Council and setting up of responsible Government in Manipur was submitted to the Prime Minister. Th. Bira Singh a leader of the Communist Party also submitted a memorandum dated 23rd October to the Prime Minister requesting for the establishment of a democratically elected government responsible to the legislature in Manipur. The tribal people of the hills also sought an audience with the Prime Minister at the bungalow of the Chief Commissioner and demanded setting up of a legislative assembly. The Prime Minister was sympathetic with the aspirations of the people and he wrote "In Manipur and Tripura, there was the demand, strongly expressed, for what is called a democratic form of government, which meant an assembly, ministry and presumably all the paraphernalia that accompanies them. The fact that they had Chief Commissioner's governing them, hurt their pride very much. I think that very early steps have to be taken to vary the present system at least.[36] Pandit Nehru further wrote "(The government) had already passed legislation authorizing the appointment of advisors. This at least should be done as soon as possible. I rather doubt if this will satisfy the people there. I think that a beginning should also be made in Manipur especially, in the constitution of a municipality, local boards and gram panchayats. That will be a sound foundation for further growth".[37] Subsequently, on popular pressure, the reconstituted Advisory Council was inaugurated by the Chief Commissioner on 5th June 1953. The new Council consisted of five members i.e. S. Krishnamohan Singh, H. Dwijamani Dev Sharma, S. Tombi Singh, Dr. Kampu and A. Daiho. The new administrative measure however failed to satisfy the aspirations of the people as it had not been delegated any significant legislative and executive power.

B. Left Wing Peasant Movement in the Valley (1948-52)

Meanwhile, there had been a lot of unrest among the Manipuri peasants also. As early as 1948-49, the District Organising Committee (DOC) of the Communist Party of India (CPI), and the Red Guard or armed wing of the party having decided to launch armed peasant revolt under the political resolution of the Calcutta conference, 1948 undertook major organizational changes. In order to ensure unity in the village, the party insisted for the formation of 'Khul Committee' (village committee) in villages and for that purpose a constitution of the committee was circulated.[38] Every committee was to have not less than seven and not more than fifteen members. The village committee was to check 'Lou Shatpa' (change tenants by the land lords) and if a villager had been arrested, the village committee was to cultivate the land and support his family. The village committee was responsible for the overall safety of the village. 'Cells' were also set up in the villages. The cell in the village was responsible to give party directives on political and other important issues.[39] The DOC had introduced the code and cipher organization known as "Tek Sangathan" and with that the party had been successful in carrying out their activities secretly for sometime. As early as December 1948, the DOC emphasized the observance of the Tek system properly.[40] According to the system all the important members had a code name. Irabot Singh was given the code name as Jogeswar, Ng. Mohendra Singh as Guni, M. Ibohal Singh as Madhap, N. Binoy Singh as Sunil and Th. Boro Singh as Bimol.

The Red Guard became very active in the beginning of 1950 and it initially arms training to about 32 cadres. Training was given by Ng. Mohendro, Th. Boro, N. Binoy, M. Ibohal and two others who formed a 'Red Guard' council. There were 12 other sub-trainers. Training was given in a hill just behind Keibi. In Feb 1950, instructions were circulated for the formation of the 'village guards' in the village. Nine to eleven persons in a village were to form a sub-troupe and three sub-troupes would form a troupe.[41] The village guard was to acquire every possible weapons from the village like lathi, spears, home-made guns, sword, etc.[42] They would get political and arms training from the Red Guards and village committee. The function of the village guard were to assist the Red Guards in the fight against the military and police forces. They were supposed to (i) patrol the village, (ii) counter the Government informer, (iii) built up intelligence network and collect information, and (iv) to make physical arrangement like digging of trenches, blocking of roads, etc, [43] so that the enemy may not easily come or escape and also make preparations so that the enemy may not arrest anyone or extort supplies from the village.

The women of the village were supposed to treat the wounded communist cadres and resist the military and police forces from taking out food and other supplies from the village.[44]

In the early 1950's the Red Guard council decided to collect arms and launch an armed revolution against the government.[45] On 10th April 1950, some Communist members held a secret meeting at Napet village under the command of N. Binoy Singh and decided to commit series of dacoities to collect money for the party.[46] The next day a dacoity was committed at Lamlai and property worth Rs.600/-had been stolen. On 18th April, four persons, viz., RK. Ibobi, A.S.I., Iboton, Constable and two other civilians, N. Sekho and K. Babudhon were arrested at Naharup by some people and detained them for 13-15 days. They were guarded by people armed with rifles, swords and bayonets. M. Ibohal Singh, Binoy Singh and Boro Singh were involved in the incident. The four persons however managed to escape after some days.[47] After this incident the government used Military and police force to hunt out the insurgents, and in the process a number of villagers were arrested for interrogation.

In May, the DOC circulated a pamphlet captioned "Congress Ki Mee-Otpa Shashan" (oppressive rule of the Congress Government). The pamphlet, while describing the torture of the villagers in the North-Eastern Manipur in the name of searching the insurgents, criticized the editors of 'Ngashi' and 'Prajatantra' two important local newspaper for defending the policy of the Government.[48] It also charged the 'Socialist Party' for being a mute spectator when the security forces tortured the masses for a number of days from 18th April onwards.[49] It may however be noted that L. Achou Singh in a statement titled 'Socialistka Communistka Khennaba: Achou Singhgi Bibriti' published in *Janmabhumi* distinguished the politics of the Socialists from that of the Communists by stating that while the latter used violent method of struggle to bring about dictatorship of the workers and peasants the former relied on democratic forms of struggle to bring about socio-economic change in the country. Achou Singh also appealed to all the left minded people to come and struggle under the banner of the Socialist party.[50]

Because of the intensified anti communist drivers a number of important leaders were arrested. On 7th May 1950, Ng. Mohendro Singh and Th. Boro Singh were arrested along with some arms, a type writer and a cyclostyling machine from Khongmanpalli Imphal. N. Binoy Singh was arrested on 1st July 1950, from Awang Jiri village and on 7th July Nongyai Singh and Tikendra Singh were arrested from Top in Imphal East. On 10th July Tebanda was arrested from the Andro village. Meanwhile, the Government had been trying to find out the programme and policies of the Communist Party. Based on some of the documents and other literatures seized from the insurgents the officials noted in August, "the documents seized by the police from the possession of certain communist leaders have established clearly that Irabot Singh had and has a plan to create… disturbance in Manipur with a view to help his own movement. Every possible precaution is being taken to frustrate such a plan".[51]

From July-August onwards, the insurgents carried on a programme of elimination of Government informers. On 30th August 1950, the dead body of a chowkidar of Lamboi Khul was found floating in the river. The next day, on 31st August, Thanil Singh of Nongren village was killed and some day later, Gulamjat Singh of Moirang Kampu was also murdered.[52] Again in September two constables, Kala Singh and Tonsna Singh were arrested by four Red guard cadres. The policemen were wounded and thrown into Iril River, but they escaped.[53]

The state government was instructed by the Home Minister, V.Patel to take help from the Maharaja if possible 'to secure Irabat Singh'.[54] In the meantime, the party had decided to send Irabot Singh to Burma for contacting the Burmese Communist parties. Irabot had left for Burma, in the first week of September 1950.[55] The party had also decided to send N. Ajit Singh, brother of N. Binoy Singh to contact the Communists in Assam.[56] It may be relevant to point out that during those days, the R.C.P.I., Assam Branch was also interested in contacting the Chinese Communist Party through the Manipur and Burmese Communists.[57] It may further be pointed out that Tongbram Basna who was based in Manipur in the early 1950s was a communist leader from Cachar. On 27th September, Irabot wrote a letter to M. Ibohal Singh explaining that he had met and discussed with the Communist Organisers of Mawlaik, Paungbin and Thangdut which were under the People's Volunteer Organization (PVO).[58] He also wrote that he had made arrangements for the training of the Red Guards in Burma and that the route to Burma via Chindwin river was quite safe.[59]

After the arrest of Th. Boro Singh, L. Ibotombi Singh became the General Secretary of the D.O.C. Despite the imprisonment of many important leaders and the absence of Irabot, the party continued to work with radical and violent activities. K. Manimohan Singh wrote that there were seven more active leaders who could not be arrested. They were, L. Ibotombi of Naga Mapal, L. Thambal of Taretkhul, Ksh. Iboyaima of Keishampat, Y. Kula of Uyumpok, A. Nipamacha of Naharup, N. Chaobi of Uyumpok and Y. Tunal of Top.[60] In December 1950, the insurgents carried on intensive poster campaign.

Despite all these attempts, the momentum of the movement could not pick up although there were few stray cases of violence in 1951. The more striking one was that of shoot outs between a patrolling army force and the Communists at Moirang Kampu in the last week of March. In the incident, one Constable and three Communists members were killed.[61] The Government got alarmed and Himat Singh was replaced by[62] E.P. Moon as Chief Commissioner of Manipur in April 1951. The move obviously was to contain the movement. However, on 28th April, the Red Guards again attacked Mayang Imphal Police Station and wounded a constable.[63] Because of the incidents intensive search was carried on and Y. Gokul Singh, the leader of the raid was arrested.

By July 24, Communist cadres were tried under section 121 A, 122 and 123 I.P.C. On 13th July, Kesho Singh of Chandra Khong, Thangjam Apabi Singh of Ukhongsang, Tongbram Basna Singh of Cachar, T. Ibotombi Singh of Keishamthong, Thangjam Tomba Singh of Keibi, Tongbram Kundra Singh of Takhel and Miss. Thoibi Devi were discharged under section 253, Criminal Procedure Code and the remaining seventeen were detained with more charges. Meanwhile, the DOC. decided to send a group of Red Guards to Burma for training. In August, Tombi of Salungpham, Angou of Wangjing, Bira of Heirok and Lala of Yaiskul went to

Mintha, Burma.[64] Irabot Singh, along with 30 of his followers met the party and appealed to both the Burmese and Manipuris of Mintha to fight the existing Government and bring 'peace to the world'.[65] However, Irabot Singh died at Tangbow village due to an illness and the plan came to a halt.

In Manipur, the 17 accused, namely, Ng. Mohendra, Th. Boro, L. Tikendra, M. Ibohal, M. Bormani, L. Gyanendra, N. Binoy, K. Rabei, Ch. Tebanda, M. Amuyaima, Kh. Lobi, K. Apambi, N. Ajit, Th. Nongyai, Y. Gokul, A. Chourjit and B. Shamungou Sharma were tried in the court of District Magistrate. Of the 17 except for L. Gyanendra and Chourjit all were convicted with sentence ranging from 14 to 3 years of imprisonment.[66] Nevertheless two more batches of trainees went to Burma, the last group having gone in 1952. In the meantime the Communist Party of India had given up the line meantime the Communist Party of India had given up the line of armed revolution and joined the general election in 1952. In Manipur also there emerged certain changes. Some of the important Communist Party leaders like Th. Bira Singh, S. Chatradhari Singh, etc., who were arrested under Preventive Detention Act were released, and following the general line of the Communist Party of India, joined the election in 1952.

C. Socialist Party and Agitation for Installation of Legislative Assembly (1953-60)

The Socialist Party, in the meantime, was trying to take advantage of the complex political situation in the state. Indeed, the party got a shot in the arm as Rishang Keishing (Socialist) was elected from outer Parliamentary Constituency with a total vote of 23,625 defeating his nearest rival R. Suisa (Manipur National Union) who polled 18,271 in the first Parliamentary Election held in 1952.* There was also election for a thirty member Electoral College in which Shri L Achou Singh was also elected from the Wangkhei Kongba Constituency. The Congress had won only ten seats as against seventeen independent successful

* In the Inner Parliamentary Constituency L. Jugeshwor Singh (Congress) won with a total of 22,902 votes defeating his nearest rival Th. Bira Singh(CPI) who polled 13,184 votes.

candidates who contested the election on many ethnic parties like Manipur Mizo Union, Mao Maram Union, Kuki National Association, Naga National League, Paite National Council, etc. The primary purpose of the Electoral College was to nominate a member of the Rajya Sabha and it did not have any significant executive or legislative power which was the popular demand of many of the political parties in Manipur. It may be noted that the emergence of many ethnic organizations in Manipur hills indicated the inability of the valley based Manipuri middle class to reach out to the hill areas of the state a fact which would have deeper ramifications in the subsequent political process of the state.

For six months between June and December 1954, the Socialist Party launched a sustained political agitation to demand installation of legislative assembly in Manipur. On 6th June a public meeting held at Pologround, BT Road, Imphal was addressed by Rishang Keishing, L. Achou Singh and W. Kulabidhu Singh and all three of them had strongly argued for the establishment of Legislative Assembly in Manipur.[67] The "Legislative Assembly Day" was also observed on 24th June at Pologround Imphal. There was complete hartal of the market places at Imphal.[68] The Party strongly pleaded to its Assam unit that the issue of the state's integration to Assam should be dropped permanently from the agenda of the party.[69]

The struggle intensified in November-December 1954. A big meeting consisting mainly of the Socialists, Communists, Nationalist Union, and many hill organizations under the initiative of R. Keishing observed the "United Assembly Demand Day" on 20 November 1954.[70] Dr.N.Leiren Singh, whose son N. Binoy Singh had joined Manipur Communist Party, chaired the meeting. November 28, 1954 was also observed as "Manipur Day". The popular slogan of those days were 'Chief Commissioner Louthokkadabani (Chief Commissioner should be removed)', and 'Manipurda Ayin Sabha Lingadabani (Legislative Assembly should be established in Manipur)' etc.[71] As the agitation intensified, Smt.Sucheta Kripalini and Ram Manohar Lohia visited Manipur to support the agitation and courted arrest.[72] On 16 December 1954, the supporters of the party started picketing Khwairamband Bazar,Chekthong,Maharanithong,Khuyathong,etc.[73] In the next few days volunteers organized picketing at Keisamthong, Moirangkhom,Sanjenthong etc.[74] In order to control the agitators, State Police fired at many places. Despite such repressive measures the agitation continued under the leadership of L. Achou Singh.[75]

As the agitation intensified the strikers attacked the office of the Manipur State Congress on 18 December thereby physically assaulting S Krishna Mohan Singh who was in the office at that time.[76] The three leaders of the party i.e. R. Keishing, L. Achou Singh and W. Kulabidhu Singh were subsequently arrested.[77] The local press followed the details of the agitation with great interest and reported that during the agitation a good number of volunteers were injured.[78] Nevertheless, as Cheitharol Kumbaba also recorded the arrest of many political leaders[79] it may be stated with certainty that a good number of the agitators were either wounded or were put into jail. It may however be noted that the agitation could not spread to the rural and hill areas of the state. On 18 January 1955, Rishang Keishing again started picketing important areas of Imphal with 55 other members. Sougaijam Somorendro Singh a close associate of Ram Monohar Lohia also crossed the Sanjenthong with 35 members to support the picketing although the agitators were stopped by the Manipur Police. In a significant development, on 26 January 1955, "Republic Day" celebration was boycotted at Sekmai on the issue of installation of Legislative Assembly in Manipur.

Between 1955 and 1956 when the State Reorganization Commission (SRC) submitted its report to the Government of India, the local press expressed a lot of apprehension that the Commission might have recommended the integration of the state to Assam an issue intermittently raked up by the Assam Unit of Socialist Party since 1948. In a perceptive paper entitled "Manipur Kadomda (whither Manipur)", C Upendra wrote that since Manipur had experienced a democratically elected Assembly based on adult franchise under the Manipur Constitution Act,1947 there should be no reason for the SRC for ignoring the recommendation of a Legislative Assembly for the state. Upendra further pointed out that the dismal performance of the State Congress in the Assembly election of 1948 as well as in the Electoral College election of 1952 was because of factionalism within the party.[80] When the SRC report was debated in the Parliament, Shri GB Pant gave a critical view in respect of the state of Manipur and Tripura, stated that he fully appreciated the wishes of the people for giving a voice in the management of their affairs.[81] The President of the State Congress also requested the Home Minister on 15.1.1956 to "take into account demands of Manipuris for elected legislature and democratic set up while giving final shape to the SRC recommendations.[82] The Committee also acknowledged Home Minister's appreciation, announced in Parliament regarding the demands of Manipur and Tripura for having a voice in management of their affairs." Indeed, Pandit Nehru had also a fairly clear picture of the specificities of the Manipuri culture, society and polity. His familiarities of the Manipuris at Bhanubil District when he visited East Bengal in the 1930's and also subsequent two visits in Manipur in 1952 and 1953 made him convinced that the Manipuris should have a distinct political identity for themselves but with a gradual process of development of a democratic institution.[83] Though the 7th Amendment Act 1956 of Constitution of India converted the Part C state of Manipur into Union Territory from November 1, 1956 to be governed by the President of India through an Administrator. The said Amendment also provided for the constitution of a Territorial Council of 30 members to be elected on the basis of adult franchise. There was also a provision for the nomination of two unofficial members by the Central Govt. Accordingly, the general election for the parliament along with the Territorial Council was held in January 1957. The election result indicated a significant improvement of the position of the state congress and the Socialist Party, the first becoming the single largest party with 12 seats followed by 7 seats for Socialist Party, 4 seats for CPI, and 7 seats for Independent candidates. RK Mukhara Devi and Anal Akim were nominated to the council and they later on joined the Congress Party. With 5 more independent candidates joining the Congress, its strength had increased to 19 seats out of 30. H Dwijmani Dev Sharma was elected the first Chairman of the Manipur Territorial Council from September 1957-58 only to be replaced by Sibo Larho who became the next Chairman from October 1958 to 2nd August 1962. Again M. Koireng Singh became the Chairman of the Territorial Council from August 1962 to 21st July 1963 reflecting intense power struggle within the party.

The setting up of Territorial Council in Manipur although was a positive step towards the establishment of Legislative Assembly it could not satisfy the aspirations of the politically conscious people of the state. R.K.Sanahal Singh on the basis of a large number of contemporary sources has given a comprehensive account of the details of the popular agitation.[84] A committee consisting of the representatives of various political parties called 'Assembly Demand Coordinating Committee' mostly from the among the members of the Socialist Party and Communist Party of India was formed in April 1960 to co-ordinate the programmes of agitation. L. Achou Singh was believed to be the main brain behind the agitation though a good number of the Communist as well as Congress cadres also took part in the agitation.[85] On 11 April 1960, the committee had organized a mass satyagraha in and around Imphal town demanding the establishment of Legislative Assembly. All the markets in Imphal and the suburbs observed hartal for about a week.[86] Theatres and amusement houses remained closed. The struggle entered a new phase from 20th April onwards. Normal functioning of the Govt. offices, courts, including transport services remained suspended due to disturbances by the agitators. Most of the bazars remained suspended for the next 2-3 days.[87] On 25th April, the state police fired ten rounds when a crowd of satyagrahis gathered at Moirangkhom, Imphal to violate the prohibitory order under section 144 CrP.C. In the scuffle that followed six persons received bullet injuries. Eighty other persons were injured persons and they were taken to the hospital. Altogether about one hundred other satyagrahis were taken into custody.[88] Not discouraged by the developments on 27th April about one thousand protestors including women and students marched to the Chief Commissioner's bungalow, violating the prohibitory order, to urge upon the Chief Commissioner to take necessary steps for the installation of Legislative Assembly in the State at an early date.[89] In the confrontation between the agitators and the security personnel a number of students were injured in the police lathi charge. The socialist party tried to intensify the agitation by sending in a number of volunteers.[90] All bazars, shops and amusement houses observed hartal for 2/3 days as a protest against police excesses.

The Co-ordinating Committee appealed to the people to observe 1st June 1960 as the anti-repression day. As a result about five hundred agitators including women came out in procession from Uripok and Sagolband roads in defiance of the prohibitory orders. The state police initially tried to disperse the crowd by lathi charge. But, when the agitators refused to disperse the security forces fired six rounds of tear gas shells to scare them.[91] Although some of the agitators were arrested the movement continued in the next few days. The agitation however subsided. In 1963, the central govt. passed the Territorial Assembly Bill. All the elected members of the Territorial Council automatically became members of the newly constituted assembly with Mr M Koireng Singh as the Chief Minister.

D. Civil Agitation against Price Rise (1965)

Meanwhile, in August 1965 the civil population of the valley area became very restive due to unavailability of food grain particularly rice and paddy in the market. It has been pointed out in great detail by many writers that throughout the first two quarters of 20th century, the people of the state had been intermittently facing food shortages (rice) which invariably led to serious cases of food riots as happened in 1939. Even in the early 1950's popular anger were expressed against unavailability of sufficient food supply in the market due mainly to the clandestine export of rice by the local traders and also intermittent crop failure due to flood. In 1952 there was a serious case of food scarcity in the valley. Pandit Nehru wrote in 1952 "The price of rice ... only a few years ago... was Rs.10. Then it started rising steeply and reached the figure of Rs.45 or even more. This was a tremendous shock and caused great distress ... the principal reason for this was the export of 4000 tonnes of rice from Manipur to Assam."[92] M. Bhattacharya pointed out that from 1956 onwards, the Govt. of Manipur under the scheme of state trading has been following a practice of procuring rice and paddy from the farmers and either sent it to the Ministry of food or sold it by open auction. The state trading office did not actually carry on any trade but functioned as an agency for procuring rice and paddy at fixed rate out of the funds made available by the central Govt. The stocks were then sold at economic prices either for internal consumption or were issued to the Ministry of Food and Agriculture. In 1957 alone the Govt. procured as much as 88,330 mds of paddy and 29,961 mds of rice from the state farmers and issued as much as 75,000 mds of paddy and 31,347 mds of rice to the food Ministry.[93a] In 1958, the system of procurement through private agencies was replaced in favour of a single agent procurement agency i.e. the Manipur Apex Co-operative Marketing Society. In the same year about 72,000 mds of rice was procured and out of that as much as 24,732 mds of rice were supplied to Naga Hills, the balance having been stacked in the state trading godowns.[93b] Because of such policies the otherwise rice surplus state had become a perennially food deficit state and the price of food grains in the market shot up. The wholesale price of rice increased from 37.50 in 1961 to Rs. 123.06 in 1971 whereas the price of salt per bag increased from Rs. 7.04 in 1961 in Rs.37.71 in 1971.[93c]

In April-May 1965 there was heavy rainfall in Manipur valley. In June-July, therefore, the price of rice had gone up from Rs.25 per md to around Rs.60 per md.[94] The general populace in and around Imphal were very restive. The public distribution system had also completely failed due to lackadaisical attitudes of the civil administration. The newly installed Koireng Singh ministry could not feel the pulse of the people. It was in such a tense atmosphere that on 27th August groups of women from across the valley gathered at the official bungalow of the Chief Minister requesting to spell out the govt. policy on the scarcity of food grains in the market. M. Koireng explained that transporters of food grains were on the way to Imphal and therefore the people should try to get their official ration card which were under preparation. The women were on a 'Tamasha' mood and they did muster inflexible public will through their sharp tongue, courageous and independent opinion. The women were also resourceful and could get into sudden burst of explosion.[95] The Chief Minister had then gone to inaugurate the Water Supply Scheme at Singda village. Meanwhile, groups of students and youths from the nearby schools and colleges thronged at the central square near Johnstone High School and Pologround. The students' community could easily mobilise through cycle couriers and they could arrange a demonstration within a short span of time.[96] The crowd then entered the official complex of the Chief Commissioner (C.C). In the afternoon Baleshwor Prasad after consultation with M. Koireng Singh and S Angou Singh, Minister of Civil Supply addressed the women and students explaining the government policy of bringing in more food in the state. However, since no tangible solution was offered the crowd became infuriated and a mob like situation had emerged. The crowd then began to attack the C.C. bungalow and nearby security posts by pelting stones. Realising the aggressive nature of the crowd, the security forces which were under the command of Bannerji, Commandant of the 1st Manipur Rifles along with the IGP of Manipur Police fired a number of tear gas shells.[97] The crowd which mainly consisted of women and young boys and girls began running out of the Chief Commissioner's compound. In the melee that followed a good number of the protesters were injured in stampede. Ms Pramodini Devi, a student of Manipur College was gravely injured in the stampede and subsequently succumbed to the wounds.[98] When a few of the protesters continued pelting stones, the security forces fired a few rounds. In the process O.Nabakumar Singh a student of D.M. College was hit and he died instantly.[99] Outside the C. C. Bungalow, on the main road, Y.Nilamani Singh, a driver of the AIR, Imphal, who brought some students in the official vehicle were stopped by the security forces in front of the main gate of the Bungalow and he was immediately shot/bayoneted to death.[100] A large number of the protesters who got wounded managed to escape from the CC Compound with the help and assistance of some of the volunteers and reached their homes safely. But a 19 year old student of Modern College, Imphal L. Choubhal Singh succumbed to his injuries.[101] As a result of such tragic events most of the roads and markets in Imphal were completely deserted in the next few days. On 28 August some of the student activists gathered at Imphal and unanimously resolved to form All Manipur Students Union (AMSU) with Sanajaoba Naoria and G. Joykumar Sharma as the President and the General Secretary respectively (1965-67) respectively.[102] Since then AMSU as one of the active student's union of the state had been playing crucial roles in the complex processes of the socio-economic and political change of the state.

The agitators mostly youths and students strongly demanded for a judicial enquiry on the incident of 27 August.[103] Due to increasing pressure, the Govt. constituted a one man Enquiry

Committee with Asok Mitra, Additional Secretary of Planning Commission as the Enquiry officer.[104] Although the report partly indicted the State Govt. for being indifferent to the pulses of the people and also for firing without proper instruction from the concerned authority, the state Congress under the leadership of M. Koireng managed to retain the government. In fact the State Congress obtained majority in the 1967 election of the Territorial Assembly with the Congress capturing 17 of the 32 seats. However, because of intense power struggle within the congress there pursued sustained horse trading among the MLA's cutting across party lines. Continued instability of the Govt. with one Ministry to be replaced by another led to the imposition of the President's Rule on 16 December 1969. It is important to note that intense power struggle within the state congress led to the emergence of a dissident group consisting mainly Y. Yaima Singh, S. Tombi Singh, Md. Alimuddin and Kh. Chaoba Singh. These four dissident leaders were instrumental in the subsequent formation of Manipur Peoples Party which would form the government after the 1972 general election.

E. Popular Struggle for Statehood (1970-72)

The immediate spark for the resignation of Koireng Ministry, however, was the violence which occurred on 23 September when security forces fired a few rounds during the course of a public meeting addressed by the Prime Minister Indira Gandhi at the Polo ground, BT Road, Imphal.[105] When the crowd consisting mainly of the youths and students began to shout slogans demanding statehood for the state, the police personnel used repressive measures like lathi charge to control the crowd. A mob like situation had emerged. Some people from the crowd retaliated by pelting stones from different directions.[106] In the clashes that followed three people including a CRPF personnel were killed.[107] Many govt. vehicles, trucks and some private cars were set on fire by the demonstrators. Altogether 34 persons including 4 persons who sustained serious bullet injurious were in precarious condition.[108] To control the situation the Govt. of Manipur clamped 24 hr curfew. The army had also been called out to assist the civil administration. The situation in Imphal continued to be tensed in the next 3-4 days.

The State Congress which had been thoroughly engrossed in the politics of govt. formation since 1967 decided to take up the issue of the demand of statehood full scale. In a meeting held on 4-5 January at Sagoltongba village, the general meeting of the Party authorized the Executive Committee to constitute an Action Committee to frame a detailed a programme of agitation to be taken up for the attainment of Statehood for Manipur.[109] A significant feature of the agitation was that unlike the earlier form of struggle the method and the tactics of the later was an extremely well structured, non-violent and extensively well mobilized one involving different ethnic groups of the state. The leaders of the agitation cutting across party lines made extensive mobilization inside and outside the state for giving pressure to the Central Govt. for a final decision on the issue.

M. Sanjeev has comprehensively discussed how the State Congress has tried to organize popular support on the issue.[110] In a meeting of the Executive Committee along with office bearers of the Block committees a decision was taken for raising a group of well trained volunteers for the agitation.[111] Throughout the month of February public meetings were organised in different places to mobilize popular support. On 1 March about 100000 people went for a rally along the main roads of Imphal eventually gathering at Pologound at the main square of Imphal town and agreed for a non-violent peaceful for statehood.[112] In the first 2/3 weeks of March the volunteers of the state congress demonstrated in the District head quarters both in the valley as well as hill areas as a signal to continue the struggle with full vigor. On 18-19 March a good number of volunteers observed mass hunger strike.[113]

The Manipur Bar Association submitted a Memorandum on 1 April 1970 to the Lieutenant Governor of Manipur urging for fulfillment of the just and popular demand by all the political parties and people of Manipur to raise the Union Territory of Manipur to a full-fledged State within the ambit of Indian Constitution.[114] On 26 April 1970 an all parties statehood demand coordinating body was formed to jointly struggle for the demand of statehood[115] coordinating body with support from the Congress agreed to systematically take a number of bold political initiatives viz. to resign enmass by all the Municipal commissioners, to boycott all the Govt. offices with effect from 1 August etc.[116] The leaders of the various ethnic political organizations also strongly supported the agitation. On 7 May 1970 tribal leaders namely A Daiho (Ex-MLA) , Haokholal Thangjom (Ex-President Gangte Tribal Union), Stephen Angkang(Tangkhul Long), Paolel Haokip (President ZRC), K. Kakhangai (Ex-MLA) , K. Kalallung (President ZNU), SK Hrangchal (Ex-President Hmar National Union), H. Darkhuma (President Mizo Union) etc. submitted a Memorandum to the Prime Minister demanding grant of statehood to Manipur.[117]

Soon after, 20 congress municipal commissioners of Imphal Municipal Board resigned on August 1 in protest against the government policy of ignoring Manipur while granting statehood to Himachal Pradesh.[118] Along with this bandhs and dharnas irrupted in the politically volatile Imphal area of Manipur. August 3, 1970 was observed as Manipur bandh. Normal activities in Imphal and adjoining area were completely suspended.[119] Amritabazar Patrika commented "Himachal Pradesh become a full State today, Manipur may become India's nineteenth State tomorrow. There is nothing to show that the Union government ignored or rejected Manipur's case, which is almost as strong as Himachal's.[120] Under the banner of the All Party Statehood Demand Coordinating Body, the activists of the newly formed front went all out to mobilize a public opinion inside and outside the state. The Independence Day celebration on 15th August 1970 was boycotted as a mark of protest against the ill treatment against the state. As a next phase of struggle the activists carried on programme of Court arrest at the District offices On the next day 160 volunteers including many of the MLAs and former ministers courted arrest.[121] On 17th August another 200 volunteers consisting of students and youths courted arrest in three batches in front of the Manipur Secretariat office in support of the demand for statehood. The volunteers carrying their party flags, festoons and playcards shouted slogan for statehood. Altogether, about 1300 satyagrahis were arrested by 21st August 1970.[122]

Due to unanimous support from many of the opposition parties like the CPI, CPM, RSP MPs in the Parliament, Prime Minister Indira Gandhi announced at the Lok Sabha on 3rd September that the demand of Manipur for statehood had been accepted in principle by the government. With the passing of the Reorganization of North-East India Act in both the Houses of

Parliament in 1972, necessary arrangement were made for inauguration of Statehood for Manipur on January 21, 1972 and in Prime Minister Indira Gandhi inaugurated the new State of Manipur, the 21st State in India at the Palace ground.[123]

IV

POLITICS OF ETHNICITY IN MANIPUR HILLS

(I)

That there was a process of ethnic mobilization in Manipur hills during the post-colonial days has already been pointed out in the first section. It has also been argued elswhere that for a number of reasons be it power struggle (within the party/government) or the overall political myopia of the political leaders, the valley based middle class could not reach out to the problems and possibilities of the hill areas of Manipur during 1950s and 60s. At another level, it may be argued that social and political relations in the hills are fundamentally determined by the system and relations of production in the plain areas.[124] Because of difficult topography jhum cultivation, underdeveloped technology and limited means of transport and communication the system of production in agriculture in the hill areas continued to be based on the unchanging jhum or swedden cultivation with limited terraced agriculture whereas in the valley areas because of a long history of settled agriculture, improved technology and convenient trade route the system of production both in agriculture and trade had been a relatively superior one. This coupled with lack of globalizing forces during the 1950's and 1960's, the hill areas served as hinterland of the dominant economic forces of the state. The hill dwellers were thus placed at a relatively disadvantageous position as the production from jhum fields were not sufficient to meet even their food grains requirements. Consequently as Barun De stated, reduced to marginalized and impoverished group the traditional hill leaders hardly grouped with the plain middle class.[125] The educated elites of the hills not only maintained their social exclucivism but also avoided participation in the activities of the valley based civil society organization or mainstream nationalism.[126] Instead they generally espoused local patriotism.[127]

A significant factor which directly affected the life of the hill people in the first three decades of post-colonial Manipur was the nature and forms of control of forests and its resources as the latter provided their sources of livelihood. The following data would provide a broad picture of Manipur forest between 1955-56 and 1974-75.

Class of forest	*Year*	*Year*
	1955-56	1974-75
Reserved	1004	1371
Protected	2219	4171
Unclassed	2796	3823
Total	6019	14365

(Statistical Handbook, Govt. of Manipur 1975)

It is interesting to note that the total area of Reserved, Protected and Unclassed forest as per Govt. data kept on varying between 1955-56 to 1974-75 as the above table shows. Although it is generally argued that the increase in the total forest area is due to the change from the visual survey to the field survey, the above data is understandable in the light of the fact that a number of Reserved forest were notified between 1951 to 1963. The Kangpokpi Forest (notified in 1963), Tadubi Maram Forest (notified in 1952) and Dampi Forest(1951) led to encroachment in the jhum land. As a result of continued expansion of the Reserved and Protected Forest the traditional village land of the tribal lands had been intruded upon leading to a number of litigations between the hill villages and the state Govt. In civil writ petition Case No.20 of 1958, Dated 13.8.1960 between Luitang Khullakpa and other Vs Deputy Commissioner of Manipur the hon'ble judge had given the judgment that the acquisition of 18 Paris and $^1/_2$ sangams of paddy land from the villagers of Luitang village for construction of Litan-Ukhrul Road should be considered under the Land Acquisition Act I of 1894 and therefore proper notice be issued to the Luitang villagers (as land owners) whose land had been included in the Schedule of Villages under the Manipur State Hill Peoples Regulations 1947.[128] Despite giving compensation to the land owners such cases of encroachment on jhum/terraced fields directly affected the livelihood of the hill people.

Secondly, it can be pointed out that the state forest department had for long been functioning merely as machineries for collection of taxes rather than taking up any developmental activities. During the 1960s, there were 17 approved forest contractors who were allotted 15 forest mahals and these forests mahals were subjected to indiscriminate exploitation between 1965-6. Seven contractors viz. (1) AK Bhattacharjee, Nowgong (2) Murlidhar Agarwala, Thangal Bazar, (3) PN Chatterjee, Calcutta (4) M/s Shah Traders, Thangal Bazar, (5) M/s Shah Traders, Thangal Bazar, (6) PN Chatterjee, Calcutta and (7) K. Monomohan Singh, Moirangkhom were given exclusive right for collection of Dalchini (Cinnamomum obtusifolium) from Mahal No.I, II, III, V,VI, IV, and VII respectively. Shongkao Khullakpa of Shongkao Village and Kh. Ibomcha Singh, Kwakeithel were given the exclusive right for collection of lime stone from Shongkao Lime Pits I & II respectively and Alim Uddin Mazumdar, Silchar was given exclusive right for collection of Agar woods from Jiri Barak Drainage Forests of Manipur. K. Monomohan Singh, Moirangkhom, Imphal was also given exclusive right for cutting and extracting Khangra & Yangou trees for establishment of a Ply-wood factory. Six other contractors viz., (1) Tahir Ali Laskar, Cachar (2) Sirajul Laskar Cachar, (3) Hafi Uddin Choudhuri, Cachar, (4) Alim Uddin Mazumdar, Silchar, (5) Jamkam Kipgen, IT Road and (6) M. Jatra Singh, Lamjaotongba Sagolband were given exclusive right for extraction of timbers from Block No.M.I(b), M.II, M.III, M.XII, XIV and XV respectively.[129] Although the total value of the seventeen contract work amounted to Rs. 3,03,678/- and the total revenue paid to the Government was Rs. 1,33,910/-[130], there were no significant forest development cum conservation programme were taken up by the Government. Since the department normally lease out forest areas to registered forest contractors without proper knowledge of the lower grade forest officials who in fact were habitual absentees the sale proceeds were conducted in the safe urban/town centres. The people, therefore, were hardly aware of the fact that hill forests have been sold to contractors who were free to exploit their forest. But the contractors were equally conscious and they had always involved some local people or paid agents. Thus, the hill people were under severe economic strains which was fully utilized by the emerging intermediary middle class even to propagate their ideas and interests.

When Manipur became a Part C state and was put under central rule through a Chief Commissioner, many of the missionary educated elites of Manipur Hills both from the Naga and the Kuki constellation felt absolutely suffocated although quite a few of the them including R Khathing (Tangkhul Naga), T.C. Tiankham(Paite), were accommodated in the new bureaucratic structure. It may be interesting to note that the Christian population of Manipur Hills who were given basic knowledge on catechism and religious education increased from 68394 in 1951 to 152043 in 1961. The number of school and college going students during this period also increased considerably.[131] In terms of their ideas and activities the hill elites of Manipur were broadly divided into two groups during the post independence period. A liberal group joined various local and national political parties and went along with the state politics where as a more radical group went along with either the Pan Naga or Pan Kuki-Chin politics crossing even the boundary of the State.

A. Naga Politics(1948-72)

(a)As early as 1946, Athiko-Daiho, a Mao Naga from Mao village just adjacent to the Naga hills, circulated a document entitled "My views on the tendency of future hill administration of Manipur, or demand of the Hill general public" dated 5th September 1946.[132] The document was addressed to some important leaders of the Hill communities like Z Phizo, President, NNC, TC Tiankham, Speaker, first State Assembly (1948), R Suisa, member of the first Assembly (1948), Chikhong Kabui, Mono Moyon and T. Aliba - all important leaders of their respective communities. While highlighting the differences in the developmental level of the hills and the plain regions in politics, economy, education and religion, the document argued that the hill people in order to avoid any form of exploitations from the plain men should go for a political administrative union with other hill state. He further demanded that the opinion of the hill people should be ascertained through the representatives of the hill people on a plebiscite.[133] However, he was conciliated after he was inducted in the 1947 Constitution Making Committee of the erstwhile native state. He was also elected in 1948 election of the first State Assembly. Although the Mao

Nagas once again launched a 'no-tax' campaign against the then government demanding the merger of Nagas areas with Assam as their other brethren were already there, the agitation was brought under control when Daiho and a few other leaders were arrested in September 1948.

(b) The centre of Naga politics then shifted to Ukhrul, the home of the **Tangkhul Nagas**. Under the initiative of Rev. Pettigrew an evangelist of the American Baptist Mission, the Tangkhuls during the first half of the 20th century, had evolved as one of the most modernized tribal community in Manipur. As early as 1925, the 'Tangkhul Long' (an intra tribal organization) was established in order to meet cases arisen out of inter village and inter clan conflicts relating to customary laws and the other rites and rituals. Between 1950 and 1955 while Rishang Keishing, a leader of Socialist Party (SP) was actively involved in the struggle for the democratization of politics in Manipur, many educated Tangkhuls started working in the neighbouring states of Nagaland and the Khasi Hills. As stated elsewhere, in 1952, in spite of a boycott call of the general election issued by the NNC, R.Keishing supported by a number of Tangkhul Chiefs successfully defeated his nearest rival R.Suisa (Manipur National Union) with a huge margin in the outer parliamentary constituency and became the member of the first Lok Sabha. Between 1952 and 1960, R.Keishing not only raised the issue of installation of Legislative assembly in Manipur in the Lok Sabha but also undertook intense mass mobilization programmes in Manipur hills to support the then ongoing popular agitation for the introduction of Legislative Assembly in Manipur. In the next general election held in 1957 the seat was won by R. Suisa, a sympathizer of the NNC of Naga hills. Although Suisa had contested on Congress ticket, he was instrumental in organizing the first Manipuri Naga Council (MNC) to build up the basis for a Pan Naga movement. In a significant development the convention resolved to demand unification of all the Naga tribes in Manipur.[134] A few weeks after the Convention Angal Anal, Vice President of the convention issued a statement, stressing the need for having an understanding with Z. Phizo.[135] In the 2nd Convention of the MNC, the members with a view to win the support of the Tangkhul Chiefs strongly denounced the Manipur Village Authority Act 1956 which provided rooms for an elected village council and pleaded for the return to the earlier village political system.[136] In a significant development the Convention also resolved to affiliate many Naga tribes like the 'Anal Union', Mao Maram Union', the 'Zeliangrongs' and the 'Tangkhul Long' into the council.[137] With this an extremely interesting and dynamic process of Naga ethnic expansionism had been set into motion. Indeed, in a very short period of time many of the old tribes which belonged to the 'old Kukis' with Kuki-Chin language like Anal, Moyon, Monsang etc began to be identified with the Nagas. R.Suisa along with his Secretary Z.Ramyo and Th.Muivaih were gradually drawn into the politics of NNC.[138] R.Suisa became directly involved with the 'Naga Peace Mission' and he was one of the members who went to England to meet Z. Phizo who by that time had taken political asylum in England. In his booklet, "My Legacy", he openly pleaded to resolve the Naga problem through a peaceful dialogue with the Govt. of India and began to make open demands for the integration of Naga inhabited areas into Nagaland.[139]

During those days the moderate Tangkhuls under Rishang Keishing was actively involved in the political campaign for election to the Territorial Council from Ukhrul Constituency on the Socialist Party ticket. However, during his tenure as a member of the Territorial Council, R.Keishing began to change his political stance particularly after the formal signing of 1960 Delhi Agreement. As Naga Hills was merged with Tuenshang area to be accorded the status of full-fledged state in 1963 (Nagaland), many educated Nagas of Manipur were attracted by the opportunities in the newly established state. Therefore, many of them looked upon the demand of the NNC to integrate the Naga inhabited areas of Manipur into Nagaland as a good opportunity. Rishang Keishing who was elected to the Territorial Council of Manipur in 1957 became thoroughly disillusioned with the intense power struggle within the Territorial Council for selection of the Chairmanship. It should however be noted that the 1956 Village Authority Act which aimed to replace the customary village council by that of an elected body and 1957 Act for Acquisition of Chief's Rights which directly attacked the rights and privileges of the traditional chiefs alienated a large number of tribal chiefs and other member of the village council. Rishang Keishing therefore formed the United Naga Integration

Council (UNIC) in 1967 with himself as the General Secretary. It may be relevant to note in this context that many of the Tangkhul chiefs were also alienated by the 'Hill Areas Acquisition of Chief Rights Act, 1967' which attempted to curb the customary power and authority of the village chiefs.

In a memorandum dated 19th April 1968 submitted by R. Keishing etc. the petitioners argued that the Manipur Government carried on mal administration and exploitation of hill people. The 30% reservation of Cadre III and IV services under the Government was argued to have never been adhered to since all the heads of departments were plain Meiteis. The Manipur Government was also charged for misusing the funds meant for tribal development. The extension of Indian Forest Act to the hill areas of Manipur, the Acquisition of the Chief's Right Act, and the attempt to extend the Manipur Land Revenue Act were pointed out to be crucial factors for underdevelopment of hill areas of Manipur. The Naga Integration Council therefore demanded merger of Naga inhabited areas of Manipur with Nagaland.[140] It is further pointed out that since more employment opportunities could be afforded by the neighbouring state than the parent state, the people of the area particularly, the intelligentsia chose integration of the contiguous Naga Area with Nagaland, where better facilities and amenities are available and therefore ways should be prepared to bring all the areas inhabited by the Nagas into one integrated state.

Meanwhile in 1964 the Govt. of India had entered into an agreement with the armed NNC to suspend all forms of military operation in Nagaland including some Naga inhabited areas of Manipur. Many political parties in Manipur particularly, the Territorial Congress Committee between 1964-1969 consistently demanded that the suspension of operation should cease to be operational in Naga inhabited areas of Manipur Hills as it tantamount to infringement into the authority of the state. A. Daiho while stating that Manipuri language was not only for Meitei community but also lingua-franca of other tribes of Manipur had categorically argued that the suspension of operation between the Govt. of India and the NNC was without the knowledge of Manipur Government 'the Naga underground leaders be released from the Imphal Jail'[141] The MTCC issued a publication stating that taking opportunity of the suspension of operation the Naga insurgents crossed over Pakistan and smuggled arms for intensifying their subversive activities. It was further pointed out that the Naga insurgents in order to strengthen their hold over the common Nagas had resulted to terrorizing the civil population specially the hill chiefs who refused to pay illegal levies and submit to their illegal courts.[142] The MTCC submitted a memorandum to the Home Minister Gulzarilal Nanda on 25-6-1965 when he visited the State stating that the free hand given to the insurgents under the cover of suspension of operation was a clear example of paying premium to violence and had encouraged other section of people towards the cult of violence. It was further stated that it might be difficult for the people to tolerate excesses committed by the hostiles'.[143] A meeting of the Executive Committee of the MTCC attended by many of the hill MLAs including S. Larho(Speaker), L. Solomon (Finance Minister), D. Kipgen (Chairman Hill Standing Committee), Goukhenpao (Medical Minister), P. Haokip and K. Kakhangai held on 2 April 1968 took serious note of demand of Nagaland Nationalist Party for merger of three sub-divisions of Manipur in Nagaland and unanimously resolved as "The Committee would like to add that the people of Manipur feels very much neglected and disappointed at the inclusion of 3 hill sub-divisions of Manipur in the existing agreement for the cessation of operation without prior consultation with the local Government". The MTCC has in its various memorandums and delegation had been demanding such withdrawal of agreement of Cessation of operation from the areas of Manipur".[144] Prime Minister Indira Gandhi in a letter addressed to the President, Manipur Territorial Congress stated "the reasons for extending the agreement on the suspension of operation to the three sub-divisions of Ukhrul, Mao and Tamenglong was that the hostilities and violence had spread to those sub-divisions also. It did not at all imply the acceptance of the demand that these three sub-divisions should be merged with Nagaland".[145] She further wrote that Manipur "may rest assured that while India's security as a whole will continue to be of paramount concern, the interest of Manipur will not be sub-ordinated to the interest of any other parts of the country."[146] Indeed the Lok Sabha Election of 1971 seems to have given a final verdict to the question of the integration of Naga inhabited areas to

Nagaland. In the election that followed, in the outer Manipur constituency 3 main candidates contested. Whereas Rishang Keishing, a former Socialist as well as senior Tangkhul leader stood as a candidate of Naga Integration Council, which strongly advocated the merger of Naga areas of Manipur with Nagaland, Paokai Haokip, a Thadou Kuki contested as a Congress candidate on the platform of the territorial integrity of Manipur. The 3rd candidate Y. Shaiza a Tangkhul also contested on the slogan of the preservation of Manipur's separate status. In the election that followed Paokai Haokip wrested the seat by obtaining 30.85% of the votes polled.[147] Although Shaiza, a Tangkhul Naga had cut into the vote bank of Rishang Keishing, the defeat shows the disillusionment of Naga masses to the ideas of the United Naga Integration Council.

Because of such developments, on 4th August 1972, a joint agreement was formally reached to merge the United Naga Integration Council with the Indian National Congress with the condition that INC would not oppose Naga Integration Movement as anti-party, anti-national, anti-state and unconstitutional activity. Further, it was also agreed that no Congress member would be subject to disciplinary action on the ground that he or she may be involved in Naga Integration movement. Certain agreements were also reached for organizational adjustment:

a) Either the President or the General Secretary of the new UNIC shall be nominated as AICC member by the President of the AICC;

b) One of the UNIC members shall be made a General Secretary of the Manipur Pradesh Congress Committee (MPCC); and

c) Three members of the UNIC should be nominated as MPCC members.

Obviously the AICC had considered the earlier activities of the UNIC as only or minor deviation which could be corrected under practical compulsions. Thus a sizeable section of the Naga middle class along with their supporters among the chiefs as well as the masses was once again brought within the ambit of national and state politics.

(d) A slightly different form of Naga politics was seen in the case of the Rongmeis, Zemis and Liangmeis (Zeliangrongs) of Manipur and Nagaland. In 1961, there were 8338 Zemis in North Cachar Hills whereas in Naga Hills there were 9460 Zeliangs.[148] In Manipur the Rongmeis and Kacha Nagas together constituted 38,952 personnel in the 1961 census.[149] Although the extension of the new administrative structure in 1950s brought about profound changes in terms of roads, educational institutions, medical facilities etc., in the late 1950s, the Zeliangrongs in North Cachar hills, Naga Hills and Manipur constituted a minority community.

It was against such backdrop that the 'Kabui Samiti' which was set up in 1934 was transformed into the 'Kabui Naga Association' in 1946. The motive of the new association was to work for the solidarity among the kindred tribes. On 15th February 1947, a meeting was held in Keishamthong, Imphal, which was attended by representatives of all Rongmeis, Liangmeis and Zemis of Manipur, Naga Hills and North Cachar Hills. Although S.K. Chaobe has argued that it was basically the educated Christians of the community, which attended the gathering many other leaders who adopted the traditional religion also participated in the meeting. The meeting resolved to form a 'Zeliangrong Council' with the object of furthering the economic, social, and political advancement of this community. The name 'Zeliangrong' was adopted for the first time (Zeliangrong) with the prefixes of the three tribes. A working committee of six members with Dr.T. Haralu as President. The new association was converted into the 'Manipur Zeliangrong Union' (MZU) in December 1950 and it made rapid progress. For the first time in the history of the Zeliangrong movement, the principles of liberalism and democracy were enshrined in the constitution. While incorporating the ideas of socio-economic, political and educational development as the basic objective, the constitution also stressed the need for the performance of many of religious and customary practices of the people.[150] The Union also became very broad based as each Zeliangrong village was supposed to send at least one representative to form one "Representative body" i.e, an executive committee consisting of 21 members. Each and every Zeliangrong could become an ordinary member of the Union subject to the payment of annual fee of 4 annas.[151] In 1960, after signing the 16-point agreement between NNC and the Govt. of India, MZU transformed itself into Zeliangrong Naga Union (ZNU). The whole Zeliangrong areas were divided into nine zones.[152] At significant repercussion of such a united organization was the emergence of numerous associations in North Cachar, Naga hills and Manipur, all having relationship with the Zeliangrong became very popular. Students Union, women's organizations, sports, literary and cultural organization came to be named after Zeliangrong. By 1951-52, Rani Gaidinlu for the first time after her release from Jail was allowed to come to Manipur. She visited the Zeliangrong areas of Manipur. She continued to preach Heraka (traditional Zeliangrong religion) and fight for the cause of a homeland for the Zeliangrongs. In 1951, she met the President of India, Rajendra Prasad in Manipur and expressed the wishes of the Zeliangrongs to him.

Meanwhile many armed cadres of NNC had penetrated into the Naga inhabited areas of Manipur Hills including Zeliangrong inhabited areas of Tamenglong. They wanted the Zeliangrong and particularly Gaidinlu to support their movement although Gaidinlu was more concerned for the general welfare of the Zeliangrongs. The Nagas National Council criticized her for the propagation of Animism, which was detrimental to the Pro-Christian Phizo and his followers in the NNC. Therefore, there emerged a rift between Gaidinlu and the NNC. In 1960, Gaidinlu went underground to protect herself from a possible attack of the NNC. She was however, very particular of defending the Heraka cult which resulted in constant fights between her and the NNC. There were constant shootouts between the two groups between 1963 and 1965 and in one occasion as many as 9 members of the NNC parties were killed. She also revived the political dream of Jadonang to have a Zeliangrong homeland within the Indian Union. Meanwhile K. Kallalung of 'Rongmei Association', an organization which tacitly supported Gaidinlu, submitted a memorandum to Lal Bahadur Shastri on 14th October 1964, to unite the Zelingrongs of all the three districts and to form a district administrative unit. On 25-26 November of the same year the Zeliangrong Council in the 'Heinengkunglawa Conference' demanded the formation of one unit but to be within Nagaland. The motive obviously was to bring about a compromise between the NNC and Gaidinlu. This conference formed a 16-member committee to establish mutual understanding between the ZNU and the Heraka party. Many sub committees were started in Naga Hills, North Cachar Hills and in Manipur. In 1972, when there was a strong popular movement for the demand of statehood for Manipur the ZNU submitted a memorandum to the Prime Minister demanding the formation of an administrative unit but to be within Nagaland. But this was not accepted by the Rongmei Association. When the Shillong accord was signed, the Zeliangrong Council demanded the formation of a separate unit either in Nagaland or in Manipur. Meanwhile, Gaidinlu continued to attack Christianity and preach indigenous religion (heraka) and this was well reflected in her 1979 statement when she strongly supported the freedom of religion bill and appealed to the government to drive away the Christians from the North East India. She argued that the Christian Missionaries not only served as pockets of imperialism but also destroyed the traditional culture and religion of the natives through their bigger money power. Politically, she continued to struggle for the unification of the Zeliangrong inhabited areas into one administrative unit, and this was in tune with her demand during the Colonial days. Whether the new Zeliangrong administrative unit should be in Manipur, Nagaland or remain, as a separate state was not a matter of much concern for Gaidinlu. As late as 1982, the 'Zeliangrong Peoples Convention', led by Rani Gaidinlu herself, demanded the creation of a distinct Zeliangrong inhabited area within the Indian Union. It could be pointed out that the Rani who right from the beginning only fought for the Zeliangrongs continued to maintain her position. She was given the 'Tamra Patra' in 1972 and was awarded the 'Padma Bhusan' in 1982. Thus, the political demand of Zeliangrong middle class used to oscillate from the demand of a separate Zeliangrong administrative unit to a unified Zeliangrong administrative unit located either in Nagaland or Manipur.

V

POLITICS OF ETHNICITY IN MANIPUR HILLS (II)

B. Kuki-Chin Politics (1948-72)

(a) In contrast to the Naga politics of ethnic expansionism the history of chieftain oriented Kuki-Chin politics in Manipur is characterized by a process of 'ethnic fission' or splintering of one tribe from a related or a bigger one. The earliest association of the Kuki-Chin tribes was that of the Kuki National Assembly (KNA), which initially was a social organization of uplifting the kukis, living in different parts of Manipur. The main idea was to unite the scattered and dispersed community by meeting the growing aspirations of the people in the rapidly changing socio-economic reality of post-World War II North East Indian society. It may be relevant to point out that during the 19th century when the new Kukis migrated into Manipur hills, many of them were settled by the colonial officers, particularly Col. McCulloch among the Naga villages with an objective to contain any form of anti British uprisings. The Kukis and Nagas therefore had always harboured animosity among themselves for control over land and land based resources throughout the 19th and 20th century. It is against such a background coupled with the intrusion of the politics of NNC that the Kuki National Assembly was established in 1946 with L. Misao as the President and T. Kipgen, the first graduate among the Thadou Kuki as the Secretary. Between 1950 and 1960, Manipur hills were left virtually under the control of either the NNC or the KNA.[15]

The word 'Kuki' was a generic term used by the colonial frontier officers and anthropologists to denote any tribe belonging to the Chin-Mizo linguistic and cultural group. The Assembly, after some time, turned out to be essentially an organization of the chieftain oriented Thadou. It always tried to protect the interest of the chiefs and chieftainship system which was a core ingredient of Thadou political system. Therefore, many of the non Thadou tribes like Hmars, Vaipheis, Simtes, Paites etc were disillusioned with the KNA since the interest of the Thadous always used to prevail upon the others. The KNA was also fairly unpopular among the Kuki-Chin tribes because of its refusal to abolish 'Busun'(Paddy) and Sating(Meat) tax. S.L. Lunneh, the 2nd President of the Assembly stated that the system of Busun and Sating would be acceptable to the KNA. Obviously the tribes, which disagreed with the Thadou chiefs dominance gathered under the banner of a short lived 'Khulmi National Union'(KNU) led by Teba-Kilong a popular leader of the Kuki-Chin group. The union was against the domination of one tribe over the other and against any movements that might threaten the integrity of Manipur hills and plains. The union advocated promoting perfect harmony with the Meiteis and Naga for the benefit of Manipur and her three children Khulmi, Naga and Meiteis. KNU was however incapable of retaining the Pan Kuki-Chin group against the backdrop of each Kuki-Chin tribes aspiring to assert their independent tribal identity. These tribes began to form autonomous tribal organization i.e. the Paite National Council(1956), the Vaiphei National Organization, Gangte tribal Union(1958), Hmar National Congress(1954),Hmar National Union(1959), and the Baite National Union(1962) etc.

Between 1960 and 1965 when the Naga rebels infiltrated into Manipur hills, many of the Kuki Chin villages in Ukhrul and Tamenglong sub-divisions were seriously affected. It is against such a background that the extension of suspension of military operation against the Nagas in 1965 had been critically viewed by the KNA. The Assembly was also aware of the expanding Pan Naga movement among the old Kuki tribes like Anal, Moyon, Monsang and the Maring. It was precisely because of such a reality that Paolen Haokip, Chaiman of KNA had worked closely with L. Manaobi of Manipur Peoples Party in protesting against the ceasefire extension.

Meanwhile in 1956 the Manipur Hill Areas (Village Authority) Act was passed which provided elected elements in the village council while retaining the position of the chiefs. The traditional power of the village Priest was eroded as to be in the council, the Priest had to get himself elected. There was also constant inflow of Chins from Burma to Churachandpur district. Many of the Kuki leaders who had by then become members of the state and national policy making bodies took the developments very seriously. Again in 1967, the Manipur Village Authority (Acquisition of Chiefs Rights) Act was passed and the matter was strongly opposed by the chiefs. In June 1967 about 300 chiefs gathered at Imphal and unanimously decided to resist the new Act.[154] As a result, by 1969 the KNA opposed the implementation of the Act by mobilizing the Kuki-Chin chiefs against it. The resistance to the reorganization was so strong that the 624 villages which were notified for constitution of the council in 1961, had become almost defunct by 1968.[155] The KNA also floated the idea of the formation of a possible Kuki state. Many Kuki chiefs took up arms in collusion with the Mizo National Front which was clamoring for integration of the Kuki Chin inhabited area of Manipur with Mizoram. In a significant meeting of the KNA held on 10-11 October 1969 the members unanimously resolved to demand a separate state within Indian Union. Haokholet Ngailet, Secretary of the KNA argued that since the state as well as the Central Govt. could not protect Kukis from the harassment of the Nagas between 1956 and 1964 in Ukhrul and Chandel Districts the Kukis should be compensated by granting a separate state within Indian Union. Thus the KNA began to voice for the political integration of the Kukis and allied ethnic groups under one administration. With a view to consolidate the hold of the organization, a constitution of the Assembly was drafted in 1969 but due to the complex nature of the community, the constitution was approved in 1975.[156] The constitution has 73 articles and 7 schedules. According to the constitution, the party has many organs such as the General Assembly, the working committee and the executive committee. The general assembly is the highest and the most powerful. Its main functions are to make policy and programmes for the party, preparation of the party budget, confirmation of the central executive posts, review and rectification of the plans and works performed by the working committee and also to provide supervisions over the other organs of the party. The Executive Committee consists of the central office bearers, the elected KNA MPs MLAs and Constituency President and Secretary respectively.[157] However due to power struggle among the leaders of the Thadous and other non Thadou tribes and also due to the differences of opinion regarding the use of the term Kuki/Thadou, factionalism had crept in and in 1991-92 another organization i.e. 'Thadou Tribal Council' with Paokhosei Haokip was formed.

(b) The educated elites of the Paites including T.C. Tiankham also decided to form an autonomous ethnic organization. The Paites who inhabit the south-eastern part of Manipur has close ethnic ties with the Chins of Burma and the Bangladesh. Therefore, the Paite chiefs as well as educated elites of the community had always harboured the idea of unification of these Paite inhabited contiguous area. However, when the Paite National Council came into being in 1949 it had an objective of preserving the ethnic identity and also develops the Paite language. A third objective of the new organization was to include the Paites in the Scheduled list of the Indian Constitution. Therefore in 1953, the PNC submitted a memorandum to Pandit Jawaharlal Nehru to include the Paites in the Scheduled list. The demand was fulfilled in 1956 after the recommendation of the 10-member Parliamentary committee for the assessment of the tribal situation in north east India. In 1960, a memorandum entitled 'Re-unification of the Chin people of India and Burma' reflecting the resolution of earlier meetings was submitted to the Prime Minister of India. The Council demarcated the 'Chin Tract' as comprising the whole of Manipur, part of North Cachar hills, Tripura Hills, part of Mizo Hills and part of Chittagong and Arakan 1 hills. They also listed about 30 different groups including Paite, Ralte, Simte, Sukta, etc. The memorandum argued that all these communities were similar linguistically, culturally, physically and traditionally and therefore, they might be placed under one administrative unit. After the installation of territorial council in Manipur, many of the Paite leaders were accommodated within the government. As things stand today, the PNC leaders not interested in calling themselves as Chin or Kuki. What they want is the maintenance of a separate Paite identity within the general socio-political fabric of Manipur.

(c) Among all these ethnic based organization of the Kuki-Chin groups the Hmars had a history of strong political movement for integration with the Mizos of Mizoram. The Hmars inhabit parts of Manipur, Mizoram, Cachar, North Cachar and Tripura. In 1947, the anti-chief Mizo Union penetrated in the Hmar inhabited Tipaimukh area of Manipur. Under the leadership of Dr. Thanglung who was the first President of the Manipur chapter of Mizo Union mobilized the masses with the sole objective of merging the Hmar inhabited areas of South west Manipur with the Lushai hills to form the Mizo hill district. Thus, the Hmars launched a strong agitation for 3 years including the boycott of the 1948 election to the State Assembly, although the chiefs and other village authorities of the community for fear of losing their rights and powers supported the State Government. In the election of 1948, the chiefs even sent up their representative. The Hmars supported by the Mizo union started protesting against the collection of 'Busun'(paddy) and 'Sating'(Meat) and even went to the extent of boycotting the chief for supporting the state authorities.

However, there was a sudden turn of events after the Mizo leaders in Lushai hills accepted the autonomous hill district scheme of the Govt. of India without the Hmar inhabited area. The Hmars took the developments as a great betrayal by cognate tribe and began to develop their own dialect. In 1951, they formed the HNF. Since then they had stopped speaking Mizo language. In 1954, Rochunga Pudaite, a graduate from Allahabad University and presently President of Partnership Mission Society called a Convention at Parbung. The convention not only resolved to change the name to Hmar National Congress but also requested the Prime Minister to include the Hmars as Scheduled Tribe of Manipur. In 1969 the Congress again requested the Home Ministry of the Govt. of India for constituting an 'Autonomous District Council'. After a lull of 20 years the Hmars have formed the 'Hmar National Conference' (HNC) in 1989 in a convention held at Mizoram and since then HPC has been demanding a Hmar homeland/state by uniting all the contiguous Hmar inhabited areas of Manipur, Mizoram and Cachar. The leadership of HPC is almost entirely from Cachar, North Cachar Hills and Manipur. However, the Govt. of Mizoram has been maintaining Hmars of Mizoram as an integral part of the state and conciliated the disgruntled element by creating the 'Sinlung Development Council'.

Thus a process of ethnic fission emerged among the relatively and tribe conscious Kuki-Chin Mizo groups and such a trend is likely to continue in the future.

Post-colonial Manipur, thus, witnessed a number of political agitations as well as ethnic movements of various dimensions which were of fundamental relevance to the contemporary socio-political reality of the state. Indeed some of the cardinal issues which are germane to the development of Manipur's politics were laid by the middle class during the period under study. Even among the hill leaders, while a liberal section of the educated elite joined the post-colonial national and state politics, another section of the group indulged in ethno centric political processes. Despite such contradictory trends, it was largely due to the initiatives taken by the Manipuri middle class that after twenty-three years of merger, Manipur was granted statehood in 1972 with a 60 member Assembly. The structure of the assembly in the new set up was that nineteen seats were reserved for the hill areas and one seat for scheduled castes reflecting the general aspiration of the people. The Assembly had a permanent inner chamber called the 'Hill Areas Committees'. While the Chairman of the Committee used to be an MLA from the hills and enjoys the status of a Cabinet minister, all MLA's from the hill areas were its ex-officio members. One of the important functions of the Committee was that all laws pertaining to the hill areas of Manipur, to be considered for passing by the Manipur Legislative Assembly were first to be discussed and approved by this committee. It was primarily because of such complex legislative and administrative procedure that despite repeated attempts to amend 'the Manipur Land Revenue and Reform Act, 1960' for implementation in the hill areas of Manipur remained so far unamended.

It was also not a surprise that during the first three decades of post colonial Manipur politics a number of hill elites played significant role. Out of the two parliamentary seats in the Lok Sabha, one was reserved for the hill people. District Councils in the hills, which were established in 1971 however could not work towards bringing about rapid modernization process in the hills. As a result of the above mentioned processes whatever differences that had been there between the so called 'centre' (plain area) and 'periphery' (hill areas) had been increasingly bridged with the result that many of the top bureaucratic posts in the state were occupied by the hills-based officers. The newly enriched and affluent people of the hills had begun investing in much of the land in and around Imphal. It must also be noted that in the 1970s there were more than 30 Naga and Kuki villages in addition to many other hill people's residential colonies scattered in and around Imphal.

NOTES

1. S. Rajdhan Singh, 'Calcutta Manipuri Student Union amasung masigi dharna'(pedigree of Calcutta Manipuri Student Union, in L. Damodar Singh ed. Khonjel ,Calcutta, 1956, No. 4, pp. 17-22).
2. M.K.Vallodi, *Secretary to the Govt. of India*, Ministry of State, New Delhi no.219-p. 15-10, 1949.
3. Order issued by R.A. Singh, C.C.Manipur No.0001/C.C., 15-10-1949.
4. Govt. of Manipur (Law Dept) The Manipur Code, Part I, Imphal, 1963, p. 268.
5. M.Bhattacharya, *Gazetteer of Manipur*, Calcutta 1963 p.313.
6. *Ibid,* p. 346.
7. *Ibid,* p. 319.
8. *Ibid.*
9. E.Kunjeswar Singh "India's Five Year Plan and Manipur", in L.Damodar Singh edited, Khonjel, *op. cit,* p.14.
10. N. Lokendra Singh, *Unquiet Valley*, New Delhi 1997 pp. 182-183.
11. R. Constantine, *Manipur Maid of the Mountain*, New Delhi 1981, pp. 96-97.
12. E.Kunjeswar, *op. cit.*, p.18.
13. B.K. Roy Burman, *Demographic and Socio-economic Profiles of hill areas of North-East Indi*a, Ministry of Home Affairs, New Delhi , 1961, p .239.
14. E Kunjeswar, *op.cit.*, p.18.
15. E Kunjeswar, *op.cit.*, p.18.
16. Memo No.8597-601 issued by C.C. dated 18-11-1950.
17. E Kunjeswar, *op. cit.*, p.16.
18. Y. Yaima, *Punsigi Khongchatta*, p. 38.
19. Ch. Pishak Singh, Stock Taking, *Janmabhumi*, Imphal, dated 23.10.1950 Pg.3.
20. *Ibid.*
21. *Ibid.*

22. R.K. Maipaksana Singh, "Editorial (What the People Expect from the Centre") *Janmabhumi*, Imphal, dated 26 11.1950.
23. *Ibid.*
24. R.K. Jhalajit Singh, "Manipurgi Sarkar (The Govt. of Manipur), Editorial", *Anouba Matam*, Imphal, dated 23.9.1951.
25. Pamphlet issued by Ng. Tompok Singh Secretary, MSC dated 24.2.1951
26. Chief Commissioner's notice dated 26-2-1951.
27. Pamphlet entitled Praja pumnamakta haijaba dated 15-3-1951.
28. Pamphlet entitled Praja pumnamakta haijaba dated 16-3-1951.
29. *Prajatantra* dated 30/12/51.
30. Ngashi, dated 08/01/52.
31. Strike ki appeal issued by Hawaibam Tombi Singh of All Manipur Student Union and Kulabidhu Singh of Y.S.L. dated 14-2-1952.
32. Ngashi dated 11-3-52.
33. Ngashi dated 25-3-52.
34. Ngashi dated 4-4-52 p.1.
35. G.H.Singh, publicity officer, Govt. of Manipur, press note Ngashi 4-4-52, pp. 2-3.
36. Excerpts from "A note by the Prime Minister on his tour of the North Eastern Frontier areas in October 1952(19-25 October 1952)" in H. Ranbir Singh, 'Nehru and Manipur' New Delhi ,1989 p.33.
37. *Ibid.*
38. Khul Committee gi niyam tantra or rules and regulations of village committee.
39. Kothong local cell gi Niyam or the regulations of Kothong cell dated 10/09/1951.
40. DOC Circular No. 3 dated 13/12/1948 in the judgment, D.M. Criminal Case No. 1 of 1951, Manipur State versus Hijam Irabot Singh of Janmasthan and other 43 accused, Office of the District Magistrate Manipur.
41. Red Guard circular No. 2, Khun Ngakpagi Niyam.
42. *Ibid.*
43. *Ibid.*

44. *Ibid.*
45. D.M. Criminal Case no. 1 of 1951, *op.cit.*
46. K. Manimohan Singh, *Hijam Irabot and political movement in Manipur*, Delhi 1989, p.379.
47. D.M. Criminal Case No.1 of 1951.
48. 'Congress Ki Mee-Otpa Shashan', dated 23/05/1950, p. 2, a pamphlet issued by Manipur Communist Party.
49. *Ibid.*
50. Janmabhumi,*op.cit.*,23 Oct,1950, p.1.
51. D.M.Criminal Case No. 1/1951 *ibid.*
52. K. Manimohan Singh *op.cit.*, p. 386.
53. *Ibid.*
54. *Ibid.*
55. V.Patel's letter to Jairamdas Doulatram, dated 5.6.1950, reproduced in M. Anand Mohon Singh, Shillong, 1949, Imphal, 2004, Appendix-x, pp.122-123.
56. Bimal. J. Dev, Dilip K. Lahiri, *Manipur, Culture and Politics*, Delhi, 1983, p. 141.
57. K. Manimohan Singh *op.cit.*, pp. 388-389.
58. K. Manimohan Singh, *op.cit.*, p. 391.
59. K. Manimohan Singh, p. 395.
60. D.M. Criminal Case No. 1 of 1951.
61. *Ibid.* 398.
62. *Ibid.*
63. D.M. Criminal Case No.1 of 1951.
64. *Prajatantra* dated 27.6.1954, p.1.
65. *Ibid.*, 28.6.1954, p.1.
66. S. Ibomcha Singh, Congress and Political Development in Manipur, unpublished MPhil Dissertation submitted to Manipur University p.161.
67. Ngasi dated 18.11.1954 p.2.
68. Ngasi dated 30.11.1954 p.1.

69. Satyagraha Bulletin published by Socialist Party, November, 1954.
70. Prajatantra dated 19.12.1954 p.1.
71. *Ibid.*
72. *Ibid.*
73. *Ibid.*
74. *Ibid.*, dated 23.12.1954 and 27.12.1954 also see L Ibungohal Singh and N Khelchandra and Cheitharol Kumbaba, Imphal 1976, pp. 678, 680.
75. *Prajatantra*, dated 22.12.1954 p.2.
76. *Ibid.*
77. "Policeki Kahenba Thabakta Athuba Inquiry Toubiyu" in *Prajatantra*, dated 11.1.1955.
78. *Ibid.*
79. L Ibungohal Singh, N Khelchandra and Cheitharol Kumbaba, Imphal 1976, pp. 678,680.
80. C Upendra, "Manipur Kadomda (Whither Manipur)" in L Damodar Singh ed. Opcit.pp.22-28.
81. Mairembam Sanjeev, Shri M. Koireng Gee Punshi Amasung Thabak, (Imphal 2010), p.72.
82. Quoted in Mairembam Sanjeev "Shri M. Koireng Gee Punshi Amasung Thabak", (Imphal 2010), p.72.
83. Excerpts from "A Note by the Prime Minister on his tour of the North Eastern Frontier areas in October 1952(19-25 October 1952)" in H. Ranbir Singh, *op. cit.*, p.33.
84. R.K.Sanahal Singh," Post Merger Political History of Manipur", in N. Sanajaoba ed. *Manipur Past and Present*, New Delhi, pp. 175-192.
85. *Ibid.*, p. 178.
86. *Ibid.*, p. 177.
87. Jubati Devi, Eihakki Punshida Rajniti Amasung Jail, T. Bokul ed. Yaon, Imphal, October 1971, No.X . pp. 23-32.
88. *Ibid.*
89. *Ibid.*

90. *Ibid.,* p.178.

91. R.K.Sanahal Singh," Post Merger Political History of Manipur", in N.Sanajaoba ed. *op. cit.*

92. Excerpts from "A note by the Prime Minister on his tour of the North Eastern Frontier areas in October 1952 (19-25 October 1952)" *op. cit.,* pp.32-33.

93a. M. Bhattacharya, *op.cit,* pp.260-261.

93b. *Ibid.*

93c. *Ibid.*

94. Economic Survey Manipur 2005-06, Directorate of Statistics, Govt. of Manipur, p 40.

95. '27th August and Mitra Commission' in A.C.Netrajit (ed.) AMSU Silver Jubilee Souvenir, 1965-1990, (Imphal, 1990), pp. 1-3.

96. *Ibid.*

97. *Ibid.*

98. *Ibid*

99. *Ibid.*

100. *Ibid.*

101. 'Adungeigi Irai Numit August Tang 27, 1965' in A.C.Netrajit ed., AMSU Silver Jubilee Souvenir, 1965-1990, (Imphal, 1990), p. 10.

102. *Ibid.,* pp. 14-15.

103. *Ibid.,* p. 15.

104. *Ibid.*

105. *Ibid.*

106. Ibid.

107. *Ibid,* pp.15-16

108. *Ibid.*

109. *Ibid.* pp.16-17.

110. *Ibid.*

111. *Ibid.*

112. R.K. Sanahal, *Post Merger Political History of Manipur, op. cit.,* pp.183.

113. *Ibid.*

114. *Ibid.*

115. M.Sanjeev, *Op.cit.*, p. 90.

116. *Ibid.*

117. *Ibid.*

118. *Ibid.*

119. *Ibid.* p. 91.

120. R.K.Sanahal Singh, ibid. p.185.

121. M.Sanjeev Op.cit.,p.91.

122. *Ibid.*

123. R.K.Sanahal,Op.cit., p.185.

124. Barun De, Mountain Rage, the Telegraph dated 27.10.2004 page 9.

125. *Ibid.*

126. Barun De, Mountain Rage, the Telegraph dated 27.10.2004 page 9.

127. *Ibid.*

128. AIR1961 Manipur 31 V 48 C 10, TNR Tirumalpad, JC

129. B.K.Roy Burman, Demographic and socio-economic profiles of hill areas of North- East India, Ministry of Home Affairs , New Delhi ,1961, Appendix XXVII - Forest contractors in Manipur, pp. cvii, cviii, cix. p.191

130. *Ibid.* Appendix X pp xxxii-xxxiii.

131. *Ibid.*

132. Athiko Daiho's letter dated 5.9.46 reproduced in the *Resistance*, Imphal, dated 1976.

133. *Ibid.*

134. S.K.Chaube, *Hills Politics in North Eastern India*, Patna, 1973, pp. 211-212.

135. *Ibid.*

136. *Ibid.*

137. *Ibid.*

138. Gangmumei Kamei' "Ethnic responses to merger: A historical perspective" a paper presented in" National Convention on Merger Issue", October 28-29, 1993, Imphal.

139. R.Suisa, "My Legacy", Dimapur,1960, pp. 3-10.

140. Memorandum submitted by the MTCC to the Hon'ble Minister Shri Guzarilal Nanda on his August visit to Manipur on 25-6-65.

141. Prajatantra, Imphal, dated 20-9-64, and 16.9.64.

142. Memorandum submitted by the MTCC to the Hon'ble Minister Shri Guzarilal Nanda on his August visit to Manipur on 25-6-65.

143. *Ibid.*

144. An Emergency Meeting of the Executive Committee of Manipur TerritorialCongress Committee held on 2.4.1968 with RK Birachandra Singh, President in the Chair

145. Indira Gandhi's letter No. Secret 676-PMO/68 dt.23 July 1968 to R.K. Birachandra Singh, President MTCC, Imphal reproduced in Lt Col RK Rajendra Singh (Retd), Integration of Manipur Vs Sixth Schedule and Other Demands, pp. 208- 209

146. *Ibid.*

147. Gangmumei Kamei, *op.cit.*

148. Constitution of Manipur Zeliangrong Union, Imphal, 1955, pp.1-3.

149. Constitution of ZNU, pp. 1-4.

150. *Ibid.*

151. *Ibid.*

152. *Ibid.*

153. SK Chaube, *op. cit.*, p. 210.

154. *Ibid.* p. 212.

155. *Ibid.*, p. 213.

156. Constitution of KNA, pp.1-6.

157. *Ibid.*

7

MIDDLE CLASS IN MANIPUR

M.C. Arunkumar

In the second half of 18th century, the neighboring country, Burma attacked Manipur frequently for two reasons: (a) to revenge for the Manipuri military actions on Burmese in the first half of the century that gave a fatal blow to Toungoo Dynasty of the Burma; (Kamei 1991), (b) to make a passage for the Burmese to Bengal where East India Company Head Quarter was situated. During this period, the Manipur lost her sovereignty and regained it within a short period of time. Because of these frequent Burmese attacks, Manipur had to look westward. She had to establish friendship with Cachar kingdom, Assam and even with East India Company. For the same reason, Manipur signed a treaty with the Company in 1762 (Kamei 1991). In spite of the treaty and her friendship with the British, Manipur lost her sovereignty in 1819 in the hands of the aggressive Burmese. Unlike the previous experience, the Burmese installed their puppet kings this time. Several hundreds of people had been killed; several thousands had been captured and taken away to Burma; thousands of the Manipuri fled to Assam, Tripura and even to different parts of Bengal (now in Bangladesh). This caused serious demographic change. Manipur regained her sovereignty in 1826 with the help of British. The office of British Political Agency was established at Imphal in the same year and looked after the administration of the King of Manipur. Since then, Manipur entered into the world of capitalism with their limited knowledge and in their most difficult times.

The agreement, signed on 18 April 1833 between Manipur and British, was the first move towards the colonial rule and

Manipur's unbalanced entry into capitalist system. The Rajah of Manipur agreed not to obstruct the 'trade carried on between the two countries by Bengali or Mannipoore merchants' and not to exact heavy duties or to make a monopoly of any article of merchandise. He further agreed not to prevent 'the Naga inhabiting the Kalanaga and Noon-jai Ranges of Hills from selling or bartering ginger, cotton, pepper and every other article, in fact the produce of their country, in the plains of Cachar, at the Banskandu and Oodharban bazaars, as has been their custom' (Ganguly 2006). This agreement and the construction of road connecting Cachar with Manipur pasing 'Kalanaga and Kowpoom hills' are the landmarks of Manipuri history as these are the beginning of Manipur's transformation to peripheral capitalist society. Another landmark is the decision of constructing 'cart road' from Imphal to Kohima, headquarters of Naga Hills in 1879-80; the decision was taken while Mr Elliot, Chief Commissioner of Assam visited. In 1881 construction of the cart road from Imphal to Mao on the northern part of Manipur bordering Naga Hills was completed (Ganguly 2006).

The period is one of the most confusing periods in the history of Manipur. Politically, one thing is certain that they liked to keep Manipur as their launching pad to attack Burma. Over several points of mutual mistrusts in administration and political affairs, Manipur had no option but to enter Anglo-Manipur War in 1891. She once again lost her sovereignty. British ruled the State through a 'native' king. They crowned a minor. He was chosen by them from a different lineage line from the last independent king of Manipur. Thus, the State came under the indirect-rule, in Frederick Lugard's sense, of British colonialism. The indirect-rule is direct rule through indirect means (Lugard 1891).

Under the shadow of British colonialism, the entire social and political structures of then state changed in a dramatic way. The monetization of economy took place. The land was levied and brought a new land law. In the market, a group of traders from other parts of India came up and a trading class, mainly consisted of outsiders, came into being. They sold various imported items ranging from clothes to cycles. These traders also exported many commodities from the State to other parts of India.

At this time, the ruling class of 'Asiatic Society' of Manipur could not play any role in the newly introduced administrative structure. The monarchy and its offices in the State became functionless. Even the king and his inner core groups were subjected to trial under the British laws for various offences such as conspiracy, waging war against the state. The noble class of the then kingdom was replaced by a new class of bureaucratic officials, initially dominated by peoples coming from other parts of India, collectively termed as *Mayang* by the Manipuris. Gradually, with the advent of new breed of educated youths, passing from Schools, established by the Government and colleges in other parts of India, local peoples were recruited in British services. The Durbar members were selected from the local educated youths. They became the germ of middle class in the State of Manipur. They were considered to be 'educated' and their role model was the *'Banglali Babu'*. Many of them were descendents of ruling class of the then kingdom. They could afford to get modern education in best schools of the State and even outside the State.

The traditional market network was replaced by capitalist market. Earlier the traders were the *Mayangs* (outsiders mainly from mainland India, including Bengal). They 'imported' items from different cities of India, mainly the Calcutta, Sylhet and later the Gauhati; these traders also export various items such as rice from Manipur. lmport-export permit was regulated by the Political Agent and the Durbar under him. Manipuris, especially the Meiteis, started to take part in the trade, the *Bepari*. With the capital they had, the Meiteis could participate in the trade of 'imported' items. In the trade, the Marwaris were the dominant group; the newly emerged Meitei traders followed their footsteps. Shops, rice mills were slowly established and a number of Meitei families entered into the world of business.

Formation of Dominant Middle Class

In this paper, the author does not like to define class and middle class. However, he likes to follow the basic outlines of Michael O West's concept of class and middle class for analytical purpose. "Traditionally, the middle class is a social category consisting of those who stand between the owners and controllers of the major means of production—that is, the upper, ruling, or governing class — and those who are most directly involved in producing wealth — that is, the working class and other lower ranking social strata, including the peasantry. The members of the middle class are usually distinguished by their professional standing—which generally presupposes a level of educational attainment above the societal average—and the white-collar nature of their work" (West 2002).

The class formation in a foreign induced historical situation involves two factors emerging as decisive: the appropriation of labor and the participation in the labor process. A rich peasant, one who works his own farm but at the same time employs labor regularly, is thus to be distinguished from an agricultural capitalist who plays no direct part in the labor process but carries out production solely through wage labor.

On the other hand, a rich peasant is also to be distinguished from a middle peasant who does not regularly employ but relies on family labor for production. In the commercial sector, a trader with retail operations must be distinguished from a businessman whose activities are whole-sale. The former are members of the petty bourgeoisie; the latter comprise the commercial bourgeoisie.

As a class, the petty bourgeoisie has traditionally included small property owners; traders (as opposed to businessmen) and rich peasants (as opposed to agricultural capitalists). State bureaucracy is able to use its education, technical skills, and its structural base within the state itself to integrate into the small property-owning petty bourgeoisie by acquiring private property individually. The petty bourgeoisie thus comprised three sections: the bureaucratic stratum, the traders, and the rich peasants (Mamdani 1976). The foreign induced class structure was in the tune of peripheral capitalist system.

In Manipur, the colonial and postcolonial rules do not affect the structure in the peasantry; the economic and social impacts of the rules are obvious but the changes that take place in the production relations and its ownership pattern are not dramatically changed as we see in non-agricultural domains of the society. The rich peasants, however, become participating in state bureaucracy, trades etc. They often migrate to urban areas where they could achieve higher benefits.

This made a new order of stratification. The only easy means of social mobility in colonial Manipur was education and best education could be received by those who could afford for it. "Aspirant indigenes could do little about the first form of differentiation, but the acquisition of "European" skills - especially Western education - was seen as the necessary where-withal to challenge the political hegemony of the colonial rulers" (Cohen 1972). The well educated Manipuris, especially the Meitei, could gain the European skills in administration and had internalized the European worldviews. They were also much influenced by the Indian thinkers of freedom struggle periods; and were firm believers of Manipuri Vaishnavism. They were, thus, fitted in the foreign induced class in a colonial situation.

In the colonial period, the concept of public emerged in the political system. In earlier political sphere the 'public' was not a functional unit. Only when there was discontent in the system, the mass could raise their voice against a specific act of state. After the emergence of middle class, for its own interest, the concept of public was created. After the two women's agitations, the scope and importance of public were becoming more focused by the middle class. The public, in the western sense, was thus recognized by the State. Gradually, in the political spheres, the public became a unit and hence, the people could express their likes and dislikes on various socio-political issues. The middle class, in the colonial period, explored the possibilities of using the public for their political interests. But, the public in the colonial context could not develop in the true 'European' public. The middle class also had a dialectically opposite two publics: the primordial public and civic public. These terms are from the Peter P. Ekeh (1975). Like in many African experiences, the public could not be developed into one. The moral and social sanctions of these publics are differently developed in Manipur.

The tests of primordial public are: a) strong sense of ownership by members of its constituents who fiercely resist state intrusions other than those that are of immediate benefit; b) it is moral and operates on the same moral imperatives as the private realm. The civic public in Africa is amoral and lacks the generalized moral imperatives operative in the private realm and in the primordial public (Ekeh 1975; Osaghae 2003). The middle class could not resolve the two contradictory pulls and demands of these two publics in the colonial period. The pre-colonial pride and its location in Indian freedom struggle, on one hand, and the primordial demands and civic demands on the other hand were the principal issues in front of the middle class. The middle class could not resolve this contradiction.

Politically, the Meitei middle class which became the dominant middle class was not a homogenous and unified class in the colonial period. The currents of Indian middle class vis-à-vis Indian freedom struggle, western values and the agony of the Manipuris operated very strongly in the collective psyche of the Meitei middle class. The opposing stands of the newly emerged middle class in Manipur were seen in the context of 1939 Women Agitation (Nupee Lan). "... the Nikhil Manipuri Mahasabha, the first political party in Manipur that came into being in December 1938, did not support the Nupee Lan. The Party was dominated by the well-to-do elites and the educated middle class. The radical group in this party led by Hijam Irabot Singh proposed to support the women's movement. But, the proposal was opposed by the majority group. Therefore Irabot Singh and his supporters broke away from the Nikhil Manipuri Mahasabha and formed a new party, which they named the Praja Sanmelani" (Ganguly 2006).

This event and many others clearly show that the dominant middle class in colonial Manipur had political agenda of reforming colonial rule rather than overthrowing the Rule. And moreover, they could not openly criticize king in his inhuman rules and political indecisiveness. But, they felt themselves as creamy layer of the society and felt different from other sections of the society. In this sense, the dominant middle class in colonial era is just acting like political agent of colonial rulers. Such a situation was reported by Michael O West:

The members of the African middle class—clerks, teachers, preachers, social workers, journalists, businessmen, nurses, lawyers, and doctors, among others—shared similar personal and social experiences in the areas of education, occupations, family life, consumption habits, residential patterns, and organizational affiliations. Despite their privileged position in relation to the mass of the colonized peasants and workers, however, elite Africans were not, for the most part, wealthy, especially when compared with most white settlers. As much as anything else, the African middle class in colonial Zimbabwe was held together by a unity of purpose: its members had interests, aspirations, and ideas that set them apart from other social classes, and they were conscious of these differences (West 2002).

Manipur's entry into the world capitalist system in a colonial context was not always favorable for the Manipuris as they could not control their political and economic decisions. As the power was in the hands of colonial masters, the local people could not participate in decision-making regarding the import-export of commodities in the State. Rice was exported in large quantity mainly by the 'merchants' coming from other parts of India under the patronage of the colonial masters. They were more or less retail sellers of the goods to one or another end. The King and his men could not do anything. The market relations changed in this historical period. The capitalist economy that had been entering into the State system since the establishment of first Political Agency led towards the formation of peripheral capitalist society. We should note here that:

> The introduction of market relations, which is a pre-requisite for monopoly capitalist penetration, is not synonymous with the replacement of pre-capitalist modes of production. It rather amounts to the creation of a social formation which can be typified as being periphery capitalist, in which the capitalist mode dominates but is intertwined with communalism, feudalism, and to some extent slavery, as the case may be. Thus the vital transformation required for capitalist penetration to take place is not the replacement of pre-capitalist modes but their encirclement, the object of which is to syphon off part of the meagre surplus that is generated under pre-capitalist relations (Tschannerl 1974).

A class of contractors emerged in Manipur. They did not have enough capital to invest into large-scale contract works; but they could invest in small and medium level works including supplies. The British wanted quick works during the WW II to be constructed or supplied. In this period, a handful of Meiteis joined the contract works. Later, this group of individuals play active role in social and political spheres of the society.

The first and second generations of dominant middle class in the State had strong feelings of anti-*Mayang*; *Mayang* is a generic Manipuri term for anyone coming from Bengal and beyond. This was mainly due to the fact that the *Mayangs* occupied major administrative posts and key positions in business world of the State. Later, the anti-Mayang feeling was further ignited with the political tone of Meitei revivalist movement. The hate-feeling of the Mayang originated from the middle class was pushed backward to the early 18th century when the Meitei society was transformed into a Hindu society. However, it should be noted that dominant middle class did not subscribe the Anti-*Mayang* attitude of the revivalist. The first two generations of dominant middle class were strong advocate of Manipuri Vaishnavism. The anti-*Mayang* syndrome, on the basis of appointment opportunity and successful business, was very strong; it could suppress the internal conflict between the traditional leaders and the newly emerged middle class, between the newly emerged middle class and the masses.

After Manipur became part and parcel of India in 1949, a section of middle class strongly felt that the fate of Manipuris would be ruined and the peoples of Manipur would be exploited by the *Mayangs*. There was a brief period of Anti-merger movement in which the Anti-*Mayang* feeling was again politically blown up. The anti-*Mayang* feeling was culturally justified with reinterpretation of earlier folktales such as *pebet*. Later, the anti-*Mayang* feeling was translated into Anti-India (or Anti-Hindu to Anti-*Mayang* to Anti-India by a few) and formed parties for independent Manipur. To them, the feeling was real and overcoming the feeling was the solution to various problems, faced by the Manipuris.

The nature of middle class formation and their attitude were not changed in post-independence period too. The increasing number of schools and colleges in first two decades created new opportunity for social mobility among the masses. The ever increasing number of graduate and post-graduate not only from different Universities (both from inside and outside the State) is the launching pad for civil administration, new breed of businessmen and other high profiled professions.

The dominant middle class for higher social mobility always looked for any opportunity and the only hurdle to their venture was a *Mayang*. But, there came a point of time when the middle class in Manipur looked for opportunity outside the State. This was partly due to limited opportunity, corrupt practices and poor governance in the State. Moreover, the 'law and order' situation, arisen out of armed conflict, gave extra burden to the middle class and hence, they like to migrate or to let their children migrate to other parts of the country, even beyond. This makes the class more distant from the social and political realities in the State. Some scholars, however, think that the anti-Mayang feeling was originated from the ignorance of modern statecraft. For example, R. Upadhyay notes:

> "Manipur was merged in Indian Union on October 15, 1949 as a part C State after the departure of British. A small section of modern middle class, who emerged in Manipur during colonial rule, assumed the leadership of the state. They like other ethnic groups of Northeast India however were unable to understand the socio-political complexity of new democratic polity after Independence. They regarded the mainland political leaders as aliens and moved round the politics of their ethnic identity. Unabated influx of immigrants from Bengal during British rule and from East Pakistan after partition followed by arrival of businessmen, lower middle class and the labour class from northern India also caused demographic imbalance in the valley. Meiteis, who belonged to the ruling community of pre-British era therefore, became apprehensive of their socio-political marginalization in the new polity." (Upadhyay 2005).

On the other hand, as this increasing number also breeds unemployment in the State, many of them start looking for high ranking jobs outside the State. They aim at Indian civil services and other lucrative jobs at the national level. However, they did not have enough courage to fight other competitors at the national level. Just to get a small support base, they want some reservation. So, the middle class did pressure on government at the peak hour of India's trouble over OBC in early 1990s. Without examining the social and economic conditions which were laid down by the

Mandal Commission, the dominant middle class argued that they should get reservation as they could not get reservation in ST or SC categories. The Government of Manipur, on the pressure mounted by the middle class, had to include the Meiteis (all the castes) in the OBC list of the State. This shows the new direction of the dominant middle class; this class is no longer a progressive but self-centered and opportunity seeking class. It is not progressive in the sense that the class cannot lead the masses or generate any new ideas in the society.

The contradictory position of the class is seen when they are demanding for or having a pride of Manipuri language as being one of the Scheduled languages in India. This pride of a historically rooted civilization is again sold out when they are included in OBC, mainly consisted of the castes, exploited by the dominant groups for years. Their backwardness was due to the exploitation for ages. The benefit of the reservation was the only passion for this class in demanding the OBC status of the Meiteis. Some of them even express that the Meitei should be included in the list of scheduled tribes. The motive is same: job reservation and income tax exemption. The class no longer considers the historical root of the people and the cultural status of the Meitei. The dream of the middle class however vanished into the blue when the 'creamy layer' cut off line was introduced.

The dominant middle class in Manipur is not socially coherent. As their root is in the colonial rule and their skill is evaluated in 'European' terms, they live in a self-isolated world. They are twice far from the masses; the mass, after the politics of insurgency gains momentum, no longer see them as their leaders. The dominant middle class is no longer politically active; they are but victim of the situation which they cannot resolve or direct.

Emerging Tribal Middle Class

Census 2001 shows that the tribal population in Manipur constitutes about 31 percent of total State population; out of the total tribal population, only 5 percent live in urban areas.

As in other parts of the country, tribal middle class came into existence in Manipur in post-independence period. Prior to

Independence, there were a few tribal educated individuals who could hold government jobs; but they could not form a class as such. As many schools and colleges were established in first two decades of independence, many educated tribal youths came up. In 2001, the total tribal literacy rate was 65.9 out of which literacy rate of males was 73.2 and of females, 58.4. The least gender gap was reported among the Hmar tribe with 9.1 percentage point. The Tangkhul has highest number of graduates among the tribal peoples of Manipur. With the rising number of educated tribal youths, their occupational structure also changed dramatically.

Besides tribal development programmes, important factors that lead to these tribal demographic changes are the Reservation policy for education as well as recruitment and promotion in all the State and Central services, exemption of tribal peoples from paying Income Tax. As per Sec 10(26) in the case of members of schedule tribe, residing in area of North Eastern states, any income which accrues or arises a) from any source in the areas or states aforesaid b) by way dividend or interest on securities from all over India does not form part of total income.

The emerging tribal middle class mainly consists of bureaucratic officers, businessmen not only in the State but also in other towns of India. Majority of them, however, are in Imphal, the capital city. In Imphal, there is marked ethnic segregation of residential areas.

With the formation of middle class, the tribal-rank-societies are transformed to stratified societies. The gap between the members of the tribe becomes wider day by day. No longer is a tribe a homogenous group but a class society based on wealth, capital and power.

Among the tribal middle class, one can observe dialectics of two contrasting processes of tribalism and detribalization. Tribalism can be used in four senses following D H River: a. the state of living in tribe; b. remains in, keeping in contact with, or returning to settle in tribal areas; c. adherence to tribal values and behavior pattern; d. a category of interaction. The tribal middle class get benefits from the state because of his/her tribal status. The declaration of Scheduled Tribe under the provision of Indian

Constitution definitely brings one or other benefits. Hence, the tribal middle class always try to project their affinities with their rural tribal communities.

When the rural tribal individuals improve their social and economic position mainly due to their occupations in bureaucracy or business, they migrate to Imphal, State capital. They settle there. At first generation, they keep in touch with their rural relatives; many such families still have their shares in village land, too. The distribution of land is done by village chiefs; in many tribal settings, all the plots of land belong to the chiefs or the community. So, in order to have their share, such urban based families do not sever all their ties with rural communities. They, occasionally, visit their original villages. From the second generation, their ties with the villages become more and more distant. They are more adapted to urban life. However, they have a feeling of using 'presentable' tribal 'material objects' so that they like to show others that they have a distinctive 'tribal identity'.

Like many tribes in Africa, the tribal individuals in Manipur do not have their own plots of land. Land here is not an individual item of land which a man owns for himself and by himself. One has his rights in land in two ways: a) as a citizen of the tribe and b) one gets right to land from membership of a village and a group of kinsfolk (Gluckman 1960). In order to get his share of village land, one has to keep a contact with the rural areas. However, the urban tribalism and rural tribalism are not similar. The urban tribalism came out from the urban social life.

Another dimension of tribalism is the establishment of churches in the ethnic line. Even in congested urban settlements, there are many ethnic based churches. As almost all the tribal communities in the State became Christianized, there are various churches of different denominations associated with their respective ethnic name, such as Rongmei Naga Baptist Church, Kuki Baptist Church. The segregation is not only segregation of tribal communities from the dominant group but also from each other. The localities, lanes, roads of new tribal settlements are named after their ethnic names such as Nagaram for Tangkhul dominated tribal colony, Paite Veng for the Paite tribe.

On the other hand, we see a process of detribalization among the middle class families. Detribalization is meant either a. moving away from tribal areas with a lapse of ties with people left behind, or b. dropping or rejection of tribal values and behavior pattern. At the first generation, wives are mainly from village; many of them live in their villages. From the second generation, wives from the same class are more preferred. Inter-tribal or tribe-caste marriage is also reported among the second generation middle class families. Though there is a sense of tribalism, the middle class individuals become more conscious of their class position and its expected social behaviors.

Because of the complex political situation in the State, the traditional tribal authorities such as village chiefs play nominal roles but the tribal middle class plays a vital political role not only in their villages but also in the State politics. The traditional authority and their functions are becoming diminished or often arises a conflict between the emerging class and the traditional bodies. It is however obviously seen that, Kuki chiefs have comparatively stronger authority than the Naga chiefs. It may be due to the fact that the Kuki middle class arises mainly from chiefs' clans and the land is owned and controlled by the Kuki chiefs.

In an urbanized setting, tribal middle class feel the need of wider tribal identity as a response to dominant middle class as well as adoption of ethnic nationalism of adjacent States in North East India. So, in order to bring out a new social solidarity, they 'invent' a super-tribalism tradition of *Lui-Ngai-Ni* (for the Nagas in Manipur to mark seed sowing festival), *Chavang Kut* (the Kukis performed as Post-Harvest festivals). 'Invented tradition' is taken to mean a set of practices, normally governed by overtly or tacitly accepted rules and of a ritual or symbolic nature, which seek to inculcate certain values and norms of behavior by repetition, which automatically implies continuity with the past. In fact, where possible, they normally attempt to establish continuity with a suitable historic past. However, insofar as there is such reference to a historic past, the peculiarity of 'invented' traditions is that the continuity with it is largely factitious. In short, they are responses to novel situations which take the form of reference to old situations, or which establish their own past by quasi-obligatory repetition (Hobsbawm 1983).

The festivals, such as *Lui-Ngai-Ni* and *Chavang Kut*, were started at the State-Level in recent past. The *Lui-Ngai-Ni* festival, organized on February 15 every year, marks the beginning of the seed sowing season. "The word Lui-Ngai-Ni is derived from three Naga tribal words. Namely, Tangkhul, Rongmei and Mao/ Poumei, in Tangkhul dialect is derived from the word, *Luira* / *Luita* which means seed sowing festival. *NGAI* is a Rongmei word which means festival and is derived from the word Gan-Ngai and *NI* is a Mao/ Poumei word which means festival. So, *Lui-Ngai-Ni* is a conglomeration of Tangkhul, Rongmei and Mao/Poumei dialect. *Lui-Ngai-Ni* festival was coined in 1987. They offer prayers to the Almighty.

Likewise, the Kuki-Chin-Mizo in Manipur organize *Chavang Kut* at the State level on November 1 every year. The State-level *Kut* festival started in 1978 and celebrated its silver jubilee in 2003. Traditionally, it is performed at village level with worshiping and offering to deities of their pre-Christian days who administered agriculture. Village authority decided when the festival would be organized in pre-Christian era.

The festival is a thanks-giving feast with songs and dances in merriment and joviality for all, in honor of the giver of an abundant harvest. After all they are all Christianized; they have the pastor in place of their traditional priest or medicine man. And the 'thanks-giving' is performed in the name of Christ. Unlike the *Kut* of pre-Christian period which was organized in their respective village, now they drink tea in place of wine during the celebrations.

Such 'invented' traditions do not touch the spheres of village life. In short, this Super-tribalism is not fully internalized by the villagers. Unlike the tribalism that operates at the ethnic level, the super-tribalism operates with a higher identity of two or more ethnic groups. These festivals are organized with a strong ideology of Super-tribalism generated by the middle class. These festivals are dominated by rhetoric speeches, stage (proscenium stage, to be specific) performed traditional dances and beauty pageants. The architecture of the festivals, the space arrangement, presence of dignitaries and their sitting arrangement and speeches are far from the tribal traditions. These inventions have two functions (a) positive function of social solidarity of the Naga or the Kuki beyond the identities of several ethnic groups; (b) negation ideology to dominant State/National ideology which is based on State/ National integration.

The tribal middle class, like the dominant middle class, in Manipur depends much on the State. Their source of income, prestige and power arises from the State resources. In comparison with the dominant middle class, they are more politically or socially coherent. However, there are differences among them over their ethnic interests. These differences are overlooked when there is clash of interests with dominant middle class. So, tribal middle class is socio-politically coherent and hegemonic at ethnic-level but not at State-level.

The tribal middle class has a command to the general tribal peoples because this class is their role-model, symbol of their success and achievement. They can influence the public opinion of the tribal peoples in the State. As they depend on the State as well as have a strong base among the people, they become power-broker in the State politics.

New Middle Class

In post-1991, a new breed of middle class emerges. The Government of India started the economic liberalization policy in 1991. By the mid-90s, the private capital had surpassed the public capital. The management system had shifted from the traditional family based system to a system of qualified and professional managers. One of the most significant effects of the liberalization era has been the emergence of a strong, affluent and buoyant middle class with significant purchasing powers and this has been the engine that has driven the economy since (Phanikiran 2011). Because of their education, especially the technical education, many youths are coming up with less capital and high skill. Many of the youths settle down in various places in the country. A few of them are working in Europe, United States of America, Canada etc.

The story telling of Indian experiences of new breeds of

student who are studying in other parts of country, especially New Delhi, Punjab, Gujarat and Bangalore is really very interesting because the stories reflect their dilemmas, ambivalent attitude. They have agony over their 'unrecognized' ethnic identity in these places. "We are often mistaken as Nepalis" say many of these students. On the other hand, they have an indifferent attitude to the hard realities and the social movements in their homeland.

These stories are lived experiences of these students who take these places have far better lives than their State, Manipur. The common expression of their experiences in the 'far better States' is "Manipur has shortage of power and hence nothing is there to enjoy life". The poor condition of electricity makes these students think Manipur is just like a dark hell and the door to 'outer' world is closed as Internet is impossible for 24 hours. The road condition of Imphal town cannot be compared with those of their 'dream land'. These dream lands are their refuge as the hellish fire of hatred to their State's condition is extinguished with the undisturbed lives in these places. Is it fault of Manipur that she has shortage of electricity? The pathetic condition of three National Highways that connect Manipur with other parts of the country is often set as examples by Manipur's students rather than blaming Manipur as having such ways as a deliberate negligence of Central Government of India.

The students studying in these Indian cities will say Manipur's poor conditions are brought by corrupt State government officials. However, one will find that children belonging to families of State Government officials share higher frequency of such students. Drug addiction and insurgent groups (and their demands for money) are also mentioned by them as examples of Manipur's backwardness. To many of them, Manipur is of bitter taste for which only avoidance is the option they see.

These stories of 'brighter outside' and 'darker Manipur' are endless. When one hears these stories very passionately, the common thread of these stories is that "Manipuri identity or its past glory now transcends to higher identity of global village'.

But, the bitter experiences of the Manipuri students in their 'dream States' is also shared among themselves and with those of their 'Homeland'. When they face troubles in these dream lands, they will call for helps in the name of 'Manipuri/Manipur Identity'. But, after the tempest calms down, their image of 'dreamland' is re-build in their cognitive space.

The author talked to one of Post graduate students in a university in New Delhi. He was doing Sociology master. While discussing the perception and lived experience of these Manipuri students outside the State where they were minorities, he narrated his own experiences in his hostel:

He was in a hostel run by the University authority. Though the hostel ran a mess, many students cooked her favorite dishes in their rooms. The practice was banned by the hostel warden. But the students did. One day, he was preparing *iromba* with yongchak and *ngari*. At that time, one of his hostel mates came and knocked his door. He found his friend on the door when it was opened. His mayang (non-Manipuri, especially of mainland India) said the smell *ngari* was unbearable. He immediately replied that "You also cook things in your room". The question was not of cooking in the rooms; it was over the smell of *ngari*. They argued for a quite sometimes. Then, the *Mayang* friend went to warden to lodge a complaint against the smell. The warden came there immediately. Feeling the smell of *ngari*, he also said against the smell. "Why?" the warden answered, "We know students do cook separately in their rooms. We can tolerate it as you require extra-food. But, we cannot tolerate such pungent smell". The Manipuri student shouted at his top level, "Which smell is allowed in the hostel, then?" He alleged the warden as being racist.

Another difficulty they face in their 'dreamland' life is threat to their lives. The selectively (if not racist) committed sexual harassment on the girls of North East India by people of 'India' (meaning heartland of India) is real hurdle to those who like to settle their lives outside their 'dark Manipur'. For example, "New Delhi, Aug 31: North East Support Centre has condemned the Connaught Place Restrobar molestation and demanded law enforcement authority to act for exemplary punishment. Panic has spread across Delhi and NCR among North East Indian girls working in unorganized sectors"(Go Manipur 2010). Further the post says "Madhu Chandra, spokesperson of the North East Support Centre, New Delhi said, "Racial and gender-based violence against girls from North East India goes unprecedented in Delhi and NCR for the last five years. There is panic spread among the North East girls working in non-organized private sectors. Until and unless exemplary action to punish the perpetrators, the gender-based violence faced by the people from North East India will not stop" (Go Manipur 2010). For overcoming this hurdle, the students or other Manipuri groups in Delhi demanded that India Government or Delhi Government has to strengthen laws in order to accommodate the North Easterners. Otherwise, they have to challenge the hurdle; but, they do not confront the hurdle's attitude; they consider establishment of 'HELPLINE' is one of best strategies to cope with the situation. When fail, they need more heat to make these hurdle melted down; the heat is in the ethnic based agitation or voices from the homeland (the alternate use of homeland and 'dark Manipur' is consciously made). Because of this double standard of these groups of the Manipuri, one will see both the negation of separate 'dress code' for North East Students which they label as racist and 'raising number of admission seekers in these cities'.

The personal achievement and holding a respectable position in the society is the general agenda of the students studying outside the State. They are removed twice far from the hard realities of their society. First, their dreams are shaped by the individuals who attained 'success and achievement'; and second, their perception of lack of opportunity in the State further pushes them away from their 'homeland'. Many of them think that unless they hold a good position, they would not come back. Otherwise, they prefer to work outside the State and settle down in these cities (if one can, "in the abroad").

In the tune of the dreams of these youths, "The Manipur government will give a cash incentive of Rs 1 lakh to candidates who clear the prelims of the combined civil services examinations conducted by the UPSC and also reimburse travel expenses of those appearing for the mains"(Correspondent 2010). The Government of Manipur, though struggling to meet daily expenses in the State, announces to pay Rupees one lakhs each to anyone who passes IAS preliminary examination for getting tuition for IAS examination in Delhi. "Our aim is to encourage our youths to opt for administrative services and excel in the all-India competitive examinations. The cash incentive is to help the candidates in preparing for the main examination by attending coaching classes outside," government spokesperson and irrigation and flood control minister N. Biren Singh said"(Correspondent 2010).

This governmental incentive is just the extension of earlier middle class obsession of 'support' in the name of OBC reservation. This does not change the nature and dream of this class. Though the class is fractured with businessmen including contractors, rich peasants and bureaucratic officials, high social value is attached to the bureaucratic officials. This value is one of the driving forces for the ministers to take this decision and opposition leaders do not oppose it because they also share the same value. The State is run by the middle class and the middle class has no upward mobility. This is reflected in this government decision.

A new breed is emerging in the private establishments in home and outside. They are more concerned with their personal achievements and careers. They are less concerned with the hard realities of the society and political disturbances in the State. Some of them have strong hatred to all the happenings in the State. Inside the State they are politically insignificant because of their numbers.

The new middle class in this post-1991 period, in home and outside, more achievement-oriented. Some of them are becoming less dependent on the State and its resources. They are less hegemonic than the tribal middle class and less socially coherent. They no longer like to associate with the social and political movements in the State. They are more entrepreneur, unlike their predecessors. But, it is felt that the middle class in Manipur, both tribal and dominant, home and outside, in their collective psyche, is searching a brighter and corruption free Manipur – a healthy Manipur. The dominant middle class is not vocal; a section of the tribal middle class, however, is vocal.

REFERENCES

1. Cohen, Robin 1972 Class in Africa: Analytical Problems and Perspectives. The Socialist Register.

2. Correspondent 2010 Rs 1 lakh as IAS incentive. *In* The Telegraph. Kolkata.

3. Ekeh, Peter P 1975 Colonialism and the Two Publics in Africa: A Theoretical Statement. *Comparative Studies in Society and History 17* (1): 91-112.

4. Ganguly, Jalad Baran 2006 *An Economic History of North East India: 1826 to 1947*. New Delhi: Akansha Publishing House.

5. Gluckman, Max 1960 Tribalism in Modern British Africa. *Cahiers d'Etudes Africaines* 1(1):55-70.

6. Go Manipur 2010 Manipuri girl molested in New Delhi restaurant, Owner held: http://www.gomanipur.com/your-story/item/273.

7. Hobsbawm, Eric, Ranger, Terence 1983 *The Invention of Traditions*. Cambridge: Cambridge University Press.

8. Kamei, Gangmumei 1991 *History of Manipur*. Volume 1. New Delhi: National Publishing House.

9. Lugard, F D 1891 The Dual Mandate in British Tropical Africa. Ithaca: Cornell University Library.

10. Mamdani, Mahmood 1976 *Politics and Class Formation in Uganda*. New York, London: Monthly Review Press.

11. Osaghae, Eghosa E 2003 *Colonialism and Civil Society in Africa: The Perspective of Ekeh's Two Public*. Symposium on Canonical Works and Continuing Innovation in African Arts and Humanities, Accra, Ghana, 2003, pp. 1-14.

12. Phanikiran 2011 *India's Liberalization Era*: http://www.chillibreeze.com/articles/India-liberalization.asp.

13. Tschannerl, Gerhard 1974 Periphery Capitalist Development - A case study of the Tanzanian Economy. *Utafiti* 1(1).

14. Upadhyay, R 2005 Manipur - In a strange whirpool of Cross-Current Insurgency: http://www.southasiaanalysis.org/papers13/paper1210.html.

15. West, Michael O 2002 *The Rise of an African Middle Class: Colonial Zimbabwe, 1898-1965*. Bloomington: Indiana University Press.

8

THE MIND OF MIDDLE CLASS AND MODERN MANIPURI LITERATURE IN POST-COLONIAL PERIOD

Nongthombam Jiten

Human history has been a history of conflict. The conflict is an indispensible part of the society. It is the driving force for the social change. There were conflicts among the clans, tribes for power of supremacy. Out of the ongoing conflict in human society, the history passes through various social phases. In the course of the social conflict, literature also takes its part in shaping the conflict as well as in bringing out the conflict resolution.

One of the important phenomena that brought immense changes in the modern world is colonialism. Basically, colonialism is a term associated in particular with the expansion of the European nation-state in the 19th century which involves the consolidation of imperial power, and is manifested in the settlement of territory, the exploitation or development of resources and the attempt to govern the indigenous inhabitants of occupied lands. In the words of Boehmer (1995), colonialism is not only to exert political or economic power; it was also to have an "imaginative command" (Boehmer 1995). Further, it changes the cultures, religion, language and even the belief system of the colonized territory as well as reshapes the human identities. Moreover, colonialism is not merely the expansion of European powers but also a "recurrent and widespread feature of human history"

(Loomba 2007) in the form of hegemonic cultural and ideological imperatives. In which literature was made as "central to the cultural enterprise of Empire" (Ashcroft 2004) and "created channels for the exchange of colonial image and ideals" (Boehmer 1995), accordingly plays a crucial role in conducting a cultural authority for the colonizers, both in the metropolis and in the colonies (Loomba 2007).

To counter this colonial relationship on the perceptions and experiences, Postcolonialism becomes a new phenomenon to delve into a critical scrutiny in the modern discourse of power relations. Because of its continuity of relationship throughout the historical process and the current position of power structure, the cartography of Postcolonialism could be drawn to all "the cultures affected by the imperial process from the moment of colonization to the present day" (Ashcroft 2004). It tries to analyze the nuances and implications of its multiple, varying manifestations of colonial project and its aftershocks (Hiddleston 2009). Ideologically, it becomes an emancipatory project to develop a counter discourse to western domination and hegemony. At the same time, it "bears witness to the unequal and uneven forces of cultural representation involved in the contest of political and social authority within the modern world order... to give a hegemonic "normality" to the uneven development and the differential, often disadvantaged, histories of nations, races, communities, peoples" (Bhabha 2006).

In the context of literature, Postcolonialism could be a tool for questioning the hitherto settled notions of literary theory and practice. We need to understand that studying literature from the Postcolonial position means trying to discover what the author is saying about life from a colonized point of view. It looks outside the text to the history of the state, and then looks deep into the text for the author's opinion about the history. It highlights the "censored voices" of the marginalized by the hegemonic power centers and seeks to discover the "sunken voices" of those occupying the margins. It further questions the sanctity and seeks reinterpretation of canonical texts by reading them against the grain and a re-alignment of the epistemic grids through which literary texts and their contexts are institutionally organized (Singh 2003).

In short, Postcolonial writing means - a) to re-examine and to re-collect the lost past, b) to liberate from the colonial hangover i.e., decolonizing the minds, and c) hybridization of the past and the present or a search for a cultural syncretism.

After the assimilation of Hinduism into the Manipuri culture, Manipur became one of the most powerful independent Kingdoms in the South East Asian Region. The Kingdom could expand its boundaries up to the west bank of Chindwin river of Burma (Myanmar) and to the forest between the Doyeng and Dhunsiri of the present state Nagaland of India and also could rule the Cachar Valley of Assam by the then kings of Manipur (Ningthoukhongjam Khelchandra 1999). Over centuries, different cultures have intermingled over many struggles to form the distinctive political and cultural identity of Manipur.

The turning point in the fortunes of the Manipuri people was marked when the Burmese forces invaded and occupied Manipur for seven years (1819-1826). With the help from the British, the Manipuris could drive them out from the soil of Manipur. From this episode a friendly relation was established between the British and the Manipuris until it became an idiocy when the British with their colonial agenda tried to subjugate Manipur resulted an open confrontation from the Manipuris which automatically broke a war between the two and defeated by the British which came to be known as "Anglo-Manipur War of 1891". For a period of 56 years (1891-1947) Manipur became a princely state under the British paramountcy and had changes in the socio-economic and political structure of Manipur, furthermore, Christianity made its footmark in the hills of Manipur. With the lapse of the British Paramountcy, Manipur became independent in 1947 and a constitutional monarchy was established with the active participation of all people in hills and valley under the Manipur Constitution Act, 1947. However, the journey was shortened when it was merged into the Indian Union in 1949 and demoted to a Part C State administered by a Chief Commissioner. After a gap of 23 years of non-self governing status, ultimately, Manipur was granted a full- fledged statehood in 1972 under the Indian Constitution. Thus, Manipur became a part of postcolonial nation-state.

From the above politico-historical landscape of Manipur we can analyze that, the present state is a product of British colonialism and the subsequent formation of modern India. Therefore the modern historical experiences of the Manipuri people attempt to respond to two major influences in history – a) the structural transformation in society and the polity in the wake of colonialism, and b) the response to the relationship in the context of development of the modern Indian state, which intervened the pre-colonial society and creates discontinuities, ruptured in the collective psyche of the Manipuris by an undefined individualism nurtured by the capitalist transformation, democracy, liberal humanism, etc. (Arambam 2006). This colonial project was followed by the modern Indian state without much structural change. Out of which, a new stakeholders evolved. A modern Manipuri middle class was nurtured in the womb of the colonial society and the subsequent formation of Indian state and they were found itself at or near the seat of the state apparatus. Moreover, a new elite middleclass who got higher knowledge of English and Bengali education from British India with a new worldview had emerged and "forged a new sensibility thereby setting a seal on their break with the past" (Chongtham Manihar Singh 2003). From this social entity conditioned by the political and historical circumstances, modern Manipuri middleclass was steadily developed and literature could not remain untouched by this development.

From these parameters when we analyze the modern Manipuri literature from the Postcolonial perspective, a contestation arises on the year "1891" as the marker point of colonialism, on the dilemma over the "two past" accelerated by two school of thoughts—a) the notion of pre-Hindu society, and b) the notion of Meitei Hindu society. The first notion is revivalist in character, commonly known as "Sanamahi Movement" or "Apokpa Marup" which tried to project Hinduism as the "cultural invader" by which distorted the socio-religious lives of the Meiteis and led to the cultural in-authenticity. They strongly rejected the constructed narratives of the Hinduised myths and the cultural idioms. They devoted themselves to the discovery of ancient Meitei manuscript, pre-Hindu belief system, values, religion and culture (Naorem Joykumar 2007). The traditionalistic consciousness with a strong sense of patriotic feeling invigorate their minds to search for the root. They attempt to reconstruct the lost identity of the Meiteis as unique by de-linking the culture constructed by Hinduism.

The second notion is in the opinion that culture is not static. They have a strong belief in the impossibility of studying Manipuri culture in isolation. Rather they belief in "cultural interface". They are in the opinion that the present Manipuri culture is a synthesis of two cultures which is not merely adoption but a distinctive Manipuri way of life (Elangbam Nilakanta Singh 1993). Out of this wrangle between the two sets of idea, the dynamics of power structure develop in the making of modern Manipuri literature.

For this paper, the author has selected a few Modern Manipuri writers at random to analyze the multifaceted dynamics of the middleclass mindset which are reflected in their writings, by assuming literature as the medium of the middleclass to manifest their inner truth, and writers as one of the family members of the middleclass society since the term "middleclass" means different things to different people. The meaning of 'middleclass' cannot be defined with income and expenditure levels only. It should incorporate the social behavior of the class. Neither the author has intension to distort or deform the masterpiece of the different writers nor playing the role of a 'Shakespeare in the bush', yet he attempts to kindle an academic discourse rather than passive recipient and to encounter the conventional wisdoms in the literary circle and among the intellectuals from a postcolonial perspective.

The concept of literature has different meanings at different periods of time and different stages of culture. It is dynamic. There is a general understanding that literature is a work of fancy words, full of metaphors and similes. Nonetheless, it is a product of the changing material world and human society. Literature challenges and articulates the existing social norms. And literary works function as the agents of social transformation. As the society moves on, it is proper to examine the dynamics of literature and how the prevalent conditions of the society influence it and vice versa.

Starting from Khwairakpam Chaoba as one of the pioneers of the modern Manipuri literature, we find that, in his collection of poems *Thainagi Seireng* (Lamabam Kamal, Khwairakpam

Chaoba 1983 new edition), he expresses a melancholic strain and tries to transcend to a divine form of life which is heavily influenced by the western romanticism and its impact on Bengali literature. This is well reflected in his poems like *Awabagi Eshei, Shiba, Miyoiba*. On the other hand, Chaoba expresses his sense of patriotism and love of his motherland through linguistic-based-identity which was influenced by the concept of modern Indian nationhood. His poems such as *Meetei Kabi* and *Meitei Leibak* are the good examples. Another forerunner of the Modern Manipuri Literature, who is contemporary to Chaoba is Dr Kamal. Essentially he is a romantic poet, in his collection of poems *Lei Pareng* (Kamal Lamabam, Chaoba. Khwairakpam 1983 new edition) and his novel *Madhabi* (Dr. Kamal Singh 1997), expresses his desire of universal love, humanism, individual freedom and a closer relation with man and nature. Simultaneously, he also lamented at the fragmentation of the earlier composite society in his poem, *Thainagi Meitei Shahitya* so also belief in the philosophy of unity in diversity in his poem, *Houjiki Meitei Shahitya*.

In the same tune, Hijam Irabot, in his collection of poems *Seidam Seireng* (Hijam Irabot 3rd ed. 1996), deals with love of nature, stories from *Ramayana*, moral philosophy of Hinduism and glorification of the creation of God. This was prescribed for lower classes in the school by the then State Government (L. Damodar Singh 2008). His other collection of poems, *Emagi Puja* (revised version Hijam Irabot 2005) which was written while he was in the Sylhet jail (1941-43), though reflects the prison life, love of motherland, the downtrodden peasants and the issue of women, his readiness to fight against injustice and tyranny at the hands of the British imperialists and the feudal monarchy, yet it neither translate his writings into praxis nor give a substantive impact to the then society since it was published posthumously only in the year 1987 by *Irabot Lairik Phongba Lup, Imphal* after a gap of forty-four years which kept unpublished, apart from being one of the "charismatic" leaders in the contemporary political history of Manipur.

Hijam Anganghal, in spite of his limited knowledge in formal education, his magnum opus epic poem *Khamba Thoibi Seireng*, a composition of oral tradition, tries to rediscover the past glory of the ancient civilization by celebrating the immortal love of the two lovers (Khamba and Thoibi) (L. Damodar Singh 2008). In his novel *Jahera* (Hijam Anganghal 2004), though a love story between a Hindu Meitei and a Meitei Pangal, he tries to portrait the cultural distances in the then Meitei society in the zenith of Hindu orthodoxy. Probably, this was influenced by the unhealthy relationship of Hindu-Muslim divide in India.

A new wave of literature sprang up with Elangbam Nilakanta Singh. He published his first poem, *Manipur* in 1949 (Chongtham Manihar 2000). The poem shows the middleclass dilemma of that time. It was the year when Manipur was merged into the Indian Union. Manipur became one of the Centrally administered States. The hopes and aspirations of the middleclass and their optimistic expectations when Manipur became a part of India were unfulfilled and shattered their dreams. The poem highlights the beginning of a failed State.

"Whither the path
No unity between precept and practice
No nexus between path and destiny
Personality more valued than ideal?
Thou art questioning, O Mother Manipur"
(E. Nilkanta 1969) Translation- L.Damodar Singh

In another poem of same title *Manipur* which was written in 1976 (Joychandra 2009), he shows his mixed feelings to the existing political realities. Sometimes he has the pride to be an Indian and sometimes he is proud to be a Manipuri. His strong belief in the cultural synthesis between the two cultures of Manipur and India is depicted in this poem. Paradoxically, in his poem *Chatlashine Kadaidano Ibani* expresses his longing for a solitude place where nobody could see him except his lover. He is more concerned of his "self" and lost the collective sensibility. In his *Pukning Leikolgi Athuppada* (Elangbam Nilkanta 2000), an anthology, expresses more on romantic themes, humanism, universal love which is more or less equal with the early modern poets.

"Beyond perception of right or wrong, good or false
Something another yes something
A metaphysical voice of something afar

That also how can I know
Since amnesia befalls me of something".
(E. Nilkanta 2000) Translation- L. Damodar Singh

Contest at the political level with the emergence and intensification of armed struggle fighting against the "merger" with India has profound impact on the contemporary literature (Thingnam Kishan Singh 2005). Being Thangjam Ibopisak one of the new wave writers, in his collection of poems *Apaiba Thawai* (Thangjam Ibopisak 1969), he consciously claims Manipur as India's 'Dustbin'. It is a post-1947 syndrome that asserts the rising tide of conflicts emerging from the crucial encounter in 1949. Further, he satirizes the society with sarcasm by using a different tone of language with a sound of cacophony.

"Hey god
Do you really exist?
Reincarnation, if possible
Let me be born as a pebble
Instead of a stray-deceased life"
(Th. Ibopishak 1969)- Free translation

More radical in nature with an extreme note of anger, alienation and nihilistic approach, Thangjam Ibopishak and Yumlembam Ibomcha in their collection of poems *Singnaba* (1974), they express the middleclass psyche of the early 70s. An impact on the degradation of political, social and economic systems and their distrust on the Democratic system of India and their sarcasm at the corrupt bureaucrats and politicians are vividly depicted. Indian Racism is unveiled in their works. The majority people's attitude and actions on 'our' women are often dealt with, with various imageries and symbols. They were heavily influenced by the political movement of Pan Manipuri Youth League in the 1970s.

"Scoundrel government of the people
Democracy of prostitution
Government of prostitution"
(Thangjam Ibopishak 1974)- Free translation

However, their resistance and temperament could not be seen in their latter works. They imbibe the hegemony of the established system as the stage of "maturity" in their writings and transplant their expressions in the form of ambivalent and a new slogan of dejection and discontent of the armed conflict faced by the middleclass family become the theme.

"In this present Manipur
Be dressed in phanek only saves life!
What do you say my friend peace keepers?
Let all the male folk wear phanek!"
(Thangjam Ibopishak 2007)- Free translation

Among the short story writers of the modern Manipuri literature, M K Binodini could be mentioned for her subtle and silvery voices. Her short story *Nungairakta Chandramukhi* (Maharaj Kumari Binodini 2001) depicts the relationship of an undefined love between a wife of middleclass strata and a person of lower strata of a rural origin. In this story, even though the woman is ready to help the person without any reservation yet the frame of this story is urban centric and patronizing at the backdrop of universal love and humanism. This could be place as a reflection of the author herself who had been brought up in the Royal family.

Her novel *Bor Shaheb Ongbi Sanatombi* (Maharaj Kumari Binodini 2005) is a story of a native princess who fell in love with a British Political Agent who was posted in Manipur during the time of British colonialism in Manipur which ends in tragic. Unlike her short stories, M.K. Binodini characterizes Sanatombi as a strong person who could fight the society. She imagines Sanatombi as a liberating woman in a male dominated society by challenging the determining norms of the society. The novel is the reflection of the women who were bored and brought up from the royal family and turned to be the women of the middleclass family after the democratization of the Indian Union. Being one of the advantaged few women who could get higher education, Ms. Binodini has the knowledge of western liberalism so also the aesthetic values of the Indian culture. She tries to "adopt" the "other" culture but cannot "adapt" to the "other" which she desires. However, she gets a "culture shock" which ultimately leads to a tragic end. Even though the novel is based on the historical episode of the then royal family, the writer takes the poetic license and blends with the feelings and wishes of the elite Manipuri women.

Going a mile ahead, Elangbam Sonamani's *Hajari* (Elangbam Sonamani Singh 1998), the writer subtly injects the attitude of nouveau riche to the common people while constructing the plot of the story, the novel dwells on the patriotic zeal of the revolutionaries under the domination of the British colonialism and the hegemony of the neo-colonialism of Indian imperialism. The writer's vision in his collection of poems *Ngairi Nungbu Ningtamba* (Elangbam Sonamani Singh 1996) diverts his political foundation as seen in *Hajari*. His ideas of freedom and historical responsibility are vague and in a confused state. He is rather a pessimist. The ambivalent attitude of the middleclass and their desire to maintain the status quos of the prevailing system while talking about social revolution could be seen in these writings.

"Freedom is too far to achieve
Freedom is an abstract"
(Elangbam Sonamani Singh 1996)- Free translation

Similarly, Yumlembam Ibomcha, in his anthology of short stories, *Numiti Asum Thengjillakle* (Yumlembam Ibomcha 1999) reflects the lives of the exploited and marginalized class. Joining the band wagon, Keisham Priyokumar in his *Nongdi Tarakkhidare* (Keisham Priyokumar 2008) sketches the rural lives and reflects the victims of the ethnic clashes between Naga and Kuki of the 1990s in a humanistic framework. The tragedy is that they never try to particularize and examine the core issues of these dehumanized conditions. Instead they twist the main issue and focus at the scenic beauty of painful nature. In short, they try to represent the voices but as "imitators" with a sympathetic tone in a patronizing way.

In *Kasturi Garage* (H. Bihari 1996), Nongthombam Kunjamohon develops his story line in one of the important historical episodes of Manipur. It was in the year 1965 that the first students' uprising against the artificial scarcity of foodgrains in the market. Nobody was able to purchase. This was created by the modern capitalist businessmen in collaboration with the State. The writer, instead of looking into the vortex of the reality, dynamics of capitalism and the readiness of Manipur youth and women to fight bare handed against the odds of the history, he tries to mock at the petty things of the innocent common people. This is but humiliatingly humorous.

The scene is not qualitatively different in Manipuri dramas. Like the Elizabethan dramas in English literature, the early part of the Modern Manipuri drama was started projected by the Pan-Indian Nationalism. The plays of hero worshipping and remembering the great historical episodes in local medium which were not against the colonial interests were the initial trend of modern Manipuri drama. However, G.C. Tongbra (Tongbra 1991) and Arambam Samarendra (Arambam Somarendra 1973) were the path breakers within the trend of modern Manipuri drama even though their plays were influenced by the western playwrights and realistic model of the West. As an observer of the society, Tongbra satirizes the society with humor and wit exposed the hegemony and hypocrisy of the power centered class (middleclass) and their social prejudices through symbolic representation in his drama *Chengni Khujai* (Tongbra 1991). The inner feeling and the technique which the writer uses sometimes detract the heat of the problem posed and makes blurred the audience while presenting the hard realities.

A multifaceted personality, Arambam Samarendra, in his drama *Judge Sahebki Imung* (Arambam Somarendra 1973) and some other works, highlights the dilemma of the elite Manipuri middleclass family. A dichotomy on the two opposite ideas of thought influenced by the westernized cultural values (Phulo Babu and his eldest son Damudar) and the Manipuri cultural values (youngest son, Mohan and daughter-in-law, Aruna,) is projected. The actors' convictions tc their stance are vividly placed in this drama. His quest to retain the old heat free from adulteration and his rejection of the new cultural value is expressed in this drama. In his other dramas like *Trith-Jatra* (L. Damodar 2008), *Whiskey Bottle Ama* (Arambam Samarendra 2003) the middleclass of the prevailing society is depicted, furthermore, most of his plays are "imbued with a passionate and romantic urge for regaining a national pride and self confidence in the course of the chequered history of Manipur" (Nongthombam Premchand 2002).

Having said this, a new genre sprang up within the present trend to inject ideas, who could question the past, to the present and the future, that have not been hitherto part of, to the body of modern Manipuri literature of which M C Arun's drama, *Rajarshi*

Bhagyachandra (Nongthombam Jiten 2007) could be mentioned. But this type of writing is very occasional and we need to examine his other works if there be. Moreover, this could be a new role model in the light of Post-colonial Manipuri literature.

A changing face of the Modern Manipuri literature could also be seen in the writings of the young poets like Birendrajit Naorem, Memchoubi, Saratchand Thiyam, Lanchanba Meetei and Biplachand, etc. (Memchoubi 1990; Naorem Birendrajit 2000; Naorem Birendrajit 2008; P Biplachand 2010) more of rebellious in nature which is mostly influenced by the upsurge of the armed movement since 1980s. Unlike the landscape used by the previous predecessors they are mostly engaged in the contemporary political landscape of the society with various themes like identity, patriotism, against injustice, human right violations, and emancipation of the exploited class. Some of them are more engaged on the issue of sexual equality, conflict of ideas, corruption, the draconian acts of the Indian democracy, fake encounter, guns and bullets, so also against insurgent groups in their act of violence, demand letters, etc. Memchoubi's *Laireipakki Amambashida* (N. Tombi 1993) and *Nongthangleima* (Memchoubi 1990) depict the women characters in such a way that they are not the blind followers of men. They have extraordinary power and freedom. The poet has a strong feeling of emancipation from the patriarchalism and gender equality for an equal status. Titled poem *Androgi Mei* (Memchoubi 1990) is more of a revolutionary poem. In this poem, the writer tries to project the contemporary political turmoil of Manipur with a historical reference to expedite a war against the oppressor.

"In the meadow of Pheidabung

....

Are standing the Meitei women
Silently with their heads bent,
And conceived in their wombs
A volcano"
(Memchoubi 1990), translation- Ch. Sheelaramani

But her way of eulogizing and proclaiming the mythical characters in her other poems as the frame of reference without much critical evaluation to transform the present society is becoming a problem which ultimately makes her writings at the crossroad. The dilemma of Memchoubi is conceived by the other young writers in the form of adventurism as their style of writings with a tone of radical fundamentalism in a romantic mood. This could be seen in the works of Birendrajit Naorem's collected works *Lanthengnariba Lanmi* (Naorem Birendrajit 2000 and *Turel Nungdi* (Naorem Birendrajit 2008). The inconsistency in the thought process and his surrendering temperament is manifested in these literary works.

A writer who is contemporary to Thangjam Ibopisak, who died as an anarchist was none other than Karam Manimohan. Being a scholar of English literature, he knows the subject matter of his area. He had a good access to various historical documents related with colonial administration of the British Period. With these acquired knowledge, he tries to project an alternative history of Manipur with his most controversial collection of poems *Lamsigi Wari* (Karam Manimohan 2007). In this collection of poems, the writer provokes the conventional mindset of his readers with his unconventional stories of different historical episodes. His style of writing is beyond the notion of Western Romanticism yet he firmly believes in liberalism. His affirmation in the choice of individual freedom and the rights of every single individual is depicted. The first stage of these poems is of moral polishing specially to the degraded women of the Manipuri society after post independence. In the second stage he tries to develop an anti-thesis out of the thesis which was imbibed in the cultural dormant of the common people by dissecting the cultural orthodox as well as by (re)looking at the historical episodes of Manipur. Unlike other contemporaries of his time, one area which everyone should accept is his uncompromising consistency of thought process. His writing is unquestionably ever unchanged from the beginning to the last end of his life.

But, the argument that has been developed by him while expressing his ideas, could not become a force that would change the society and to bring out a synthesis. He himself claims that he writes for the sack of "poetic thrill" to satisfy his feeling. Even though he tries to reflect the middleclass paradox and hierarchy of the society against the back-drop of the feudal structure, the writer because of his parochial outlook and cynical criticism make limitation in his writings which lead to a lack of public influence.

The problem is that the Modern Manipuri writers could feel the social problems yet they could not fully understand the social realities. We can find detail reportage from the above literary works celebrating the richness of the Manipuri culture, language, history, and the landscape of Manipur, social maladies, crisis of the society, etc. But at the deeper level their claim to objectivity simply serves to hide the imperial discourse within which they are created. In other words, it can be placed as beautiful front of the repressed people. Hence the integrity, moral and ethical values of the writers are becoming important which needs to be examined critically. One should also remember that traditionalism in all its forms involved a specific repudiation of the notion of universalism. This excess of traditionalism could lead a society to extreme self-centeredness and ultimately to its downfall. The other school of thought which tries to generalize the social realities in the form of universal love, humanism, peace, natural beauty and projected as the mainstream discourse negating much of the cultural roots and historical memories has its flaw. These pre-occupied notions of the "two past" imbibe in the structure of thoughts and feelings of the Modern Manipuri writers, itself makes problematize while defining Postcolonialism in Manipuri literature.

The episodic and inconsistencies in the psyche of the Modern Manipuri writers make a crude and fragile travesty in their writings, which is an inevitable stereo-typical nature of the middleclass people. The contemptibly moral corruption of the middleclass developed from the past legacies that seeks wealth and comfort as the rewards of status rather than productivity is profoundly molded in the psyche of the Modern Manipuri writers to write for awards and titles for their individual benefits, which turn to opportunism rather than to explore the received narratives of the colonialism and neo-colonialism in order to unlock the granted hangovers from the minds of the people. In fact, a Postcolonial writer could examine thoroughly the total social system and also could transform the existing state of affairs with a critical assessment of the "two pass". Then the trend of Postcolonialism or the Postcolonial writers could be seen and new literature which is alternative and accommodative in the wider world view will be coming up and that literature will help to emancipate the people's mind.

Again, in the Modern Manipuri literature, the construction of a Postcolonialist identity upon and through the dislocations shaped by colonialism has hardly been a cultural motif in the creative expression, nor has it been a major concern of literary critical debate. The question of national identity has not been seen centrally in their writings to involve questions of colonial legacies, their subversion, and their transformation in the totality. The jig-saw puzzles and the new-found sensibilities (sometimes borrowed) in the writings of the Modern Manipuri writers in representing the society and the people, and the contrary nature among the writers show the problematic journey of the Modern Manipuri Literature.

Nevertheless, any piece of writing is a product of time (Boehmer 1995). We find literatures which are having a little closer to the idea of Postcolonialism consciously or unconsciously in their works if we analyze to a selected single piece of writing of any Modern Manipuri writer. However, this is not the way to evaluate. We need to analyze the wholeness of the writers' works; the writer himself/herself and the relation with the society. A serious critique of the political concepts found in literature needs to be examined. Postcolonial writing is something which is revolutionary in nature. The writer is a revolutionary and the literature which he/she writes creates revolution by responding to the contemporary situation. This brings the "national consciousness" (Fanon 2001) and solidarity by creating a social space for cultural syncretism not simply based on similarity but of "recognition of difference" (Bhabha 2006). With this observation, we can say that the voyage of the Modern Manipuri literature could be placed in an infancy stage of nationalist writings.

REFERENCES

Arambam Somarendra, 2003 *Nungshithel Amasung Whiskey Bottle Ama*. Imphal: Macha Leima

Arambam Somarendra, 2008 *Tritha Yatra*. *In* Manipuri Leela Macha.L.

Damodar, Th. Yogendra, H. Gouradas Eds. Imphal: Cultural Forum, Manipur

Arambam Somarendra, 1973 *Judge Saheb-ki Emung*. Imphal: The Cultural Forum, Manipur.

Arambam, Lokendra, 2006 *Identities, Violence and Cultural Production in the Northeast*. Safdar Hashmi Memorial Lecture, New Delhi, 2006.

Ashcroft, Griffiths, Tiffin, 2004 *The Empire Writes Back*. London: Routledge.

Bhabha, Homi K, 2006 *The Location of Culture*. London: Routledge.

Boehmer, Elleke, 1995 *Colonial and Postcolonial Literature*. New York: OUP.

Chongtham Manihar Singh, 2003 *A History of Manipuri Literature*. New Delhi: Sahitya Akademi.

Chongtham Manihar, Leishangthem Irabot, Polem Nabachandra, eds. 2000 *Kanchi Seireng*. Imphal: Manipur University.

Elangbam Nilakanta Singh, 1993 Vaishnavism in Manipuri Literature. In H Ranbir Singh, (ed.) *Influence of Vaishnavism on the Literature of Eastern India*. Imphal: Manipuri Sahitya Parishad.

Elangbam Nilkanta, 2000 *Pukning Leikolgi Athuppada*. Imphal:Raj Publications.

Elangbam Sonamani Singh, 1998 *Hazari*. Imphal: Manjit Publication.

Elangbam Sonamani Singh, 1996 *Ngaijari Nungbu Ningtamba*. Imphal: Manjit Publications.

Fanon, Frantz, 2001 *The Wretched of the Earth*. New York: Penguin Books.

H. Bihari, E. Dinamani, A. Kumar Sharma, eds. 1996 *Kanchi Warimacha*. Imphal: Manipur University.

Hiddleston, Jane, 2009 *Understanding Postcolonialism*. Stockfield: Acumen.

Karam Manimohan, 2007 *Lamsigi Wari*. Imphal: Self.

Keisham Priyokumar, 2008 *Nongdi Tarakkhidare*. Imphal: Raj Publication.

L. Damodar Singh, 2008 *Aspects of Manipuri Literature*. Imphal: Writers' Forum.

L. Damodar, Th. Yogendra, H. Gouradas, eds., 2008 *Manipuri Leela Macha*. Imphal: The Cultural Forum, Manipur.

Longjam Joychandra, 2009 *Manipuri Sahitya*. Imphal: Ashangbam Communication.

Loomba, Ania, 2007 *Colonialim / Postcolonialism*. New Delhi: Routledge.

Maharaj Kumari Binodini, 2001*Nungairakta Chandramukhi*. Imphal: Laiphangbam Somi Roy.

Maharaj Kumari Binodini, 2005 *Bor Saheb Ongbi Sanatombi*. Imphal: Maharaj Kumari Binodini.

Memchoubi, 1990 *Androgi Mei*. Imphal: Arambam Somarendra.

Naorem Birendrajit, 2000 *Lanthengnariba Lanmi*. Imphal: Writiers' Forum.

Naorem Birendrajit, 2008 *Turel Nangdi*. Imphal: Rita Library and Preservation Foundation.

Naorem Joykumar, 2007 *Presidential Address*. North East India History Association 28th Session, Goalpara, Assam, 2007. NEIHA.

Ningthoukhongjam Khelchandra, 1999 *Manipurgi Lamkhei*. Eikhoigi Panthung 1(1).

Nongmaithem Tombi, L. Joychandra, 1993 *Atoppa Khonjel*. Imphal: Naharol Sahitya Premi Samiti

Nongthombam Jiten, ed., 2007 *An Encounter with MC Arun's Rajarshi Bhagyachandra*. Imphal: Meinam Lakhon Trust.

Nongthombam Premchand, 2002 *One Hundred Years of Colonial Theatre and Resistance to it*. In 100 years of Manipuri Proscenium Arch Theatre. L.A.a.N.P. L. Damodar Singh, eds. Imphal: Department of Art and Culture, Government of Manipur.

P Biplachand, 2010 *Keidoungei Okani Eibu Taramna*. Imphal: Loumi Publication.

Singh, Kulbir 2003 *Postcolonialism: An overview*. PEGASUS (2).

Thangjam Ibopisak, 1997 *Apaiba Thawai*. Imphal: Raj Publication.

Thangjam Ibopishak, 2007 *Shrimati Tomchababu*. Imphal: Writers' Forum.

Thangjam Ibopishak, Yumlembam Ibomcha, W Ranjit, ed., 1974 *Singnaba*. Imphal: Self.

Thingnam Kishan Singh, 2005 Manipuri Literature in History. *Eastern Quarterly* 3(2).

Tongbra, G C, 1991 *Chengni Khujai*. Imphal: Mona Tongbram.

Yumlembam Ibomcha, 1999 *Numiti Asum Thengjillakle*. Imphal: Poknapham Publication.

OUR CONTRIBUTORS

1. **Professor Ghanshyam Shah** is a well-known Indian sociologist and currently he is the National Fellow in the Indian Institute of Advanced Study, Shimla
2. **Professor Gangmumei Kamei** is a historian and now National Fellow in the Institute of Advanced Study, Shimla
3. **Professor Lal Dena** is a retired Professor of History and presently working in the Department of History, Manipur University, Imphal
4. **Professor N. Joykumar Singh** is the Professor of History in Manipur University, Imphal
5. **Professor Kshetri Bimola** is a retired Professor of Political Science of Manipur University, Imphal
6. **Professor N. Lokendra Singh** is a Professor of History and the Registrar of Manipur University, Imphal
7. **Dr. M.C. Arunkumar** is the Associate Professor of Anthropology of Manipur University, Imphal
8. **Dr. Nongthombam Jiten** is a Doctorate in English literature and currently engaged in the Centre for Myanmar Studies, Manipur University, Imphal

INDEX

***